Union Jack

by

Dale Lorna Jacobsen

CopyRight
Publishing
Brisbane

Union Jack

Published by   CopyRight Publishing Company Pty Ltd
GPO Box 2927
Brisbane Q 4001

http://www.copyright.net.au
info@copyright.net.au

ISBN 978 1 876344801

Contents

FOR MY GRANDFATHER
JOHN LAURENCE (JACK) O'LEARY

Acknowledgements

Without the enthusiastic support of Les Crofton (past Secretary of the RTBU) this book would not have happened. I also acknowledge the interest shown by Trevor Campbell, past President of that union. Others contributed their knowledge. My mother, Hazel McCracken, confided many family secrets with the full knowledge they would be shared by my readers. Tim Moroney, whose father was ARU Secretary, and therefore Jack's boss, shared his stories.

Four 'old' railwaymen, with a lifetime of experience on the lines, answered my many questions and took me on a trip along the Mary Valley Line - Leon Hoffman (fettler), Dick Hook (track inspector), Don Richardson (station master) and Don Tattnell (flying gang) who sadly passed away before seeing this book in print. All of these fine men continued on a voluntary basis with the Mary Valley Heritage Railway (The Marry Valley Rattler) long after their working days were over.

I also acknowledge the writings of Kett Kennedy, Anne Smith, Margaret Cribb, Denis Murphy, Ernie Lane, Pat Towner, Marilyn Bitomsky and Lee Mylne, and Ross Fitzgerald whose words I devoured during my research.

Others have supported and encouraged me in this long project: Janis Bailey, who invited me to submit an article for The Queensland Journal of Labour History; Jeff Rickertt (my fellow-editor for The Queensland Journal of Labour History) who read the finished manuscript; Steven Lang who is always an inspiration; readers of various drafts - Linda Ivesic, Eve Scopes, Paul Milo and my daughter Liane Milligan. Thanks also to Colin Power for the image of the Mary Valley Rattler on the cover.

I particularly wish to thank Craig Munro who, courtesy of Arts Queensland, gave my manuscript very thorough attention, and Rodney Hall whose friendship and guidance I value.

Then there is Doug Eaton who has done all a writer could expect from her partner: cooked the evening meal; listened endlessly to changes of ideas; served as taxi driver – but most importantly, left me on my own while I wrote the traumatic conclusion to this story.

Prelude

I never knew my grandfather; he died too young and long before I was born. Details of his life were sketchy: he had migrated from the coalfields of Wales as a young man; had taken his bride to live in a navvy camp on the Mary Valley branchline; he held a position of importance in a railway union.

Determined to fill in the blank canvas that was Jack O'Leary, I trawled through nearly a century of records at the Rail, Tram and Bus Union in Brisbane. A fascinating tale of political intrigue emerged that reached to the very top of the Australian government.

My grandfather and his union - the Australian Railways Union (forerunner of the RTBU) - had, by remaining true to their ideology, played a major role in bringing corrupt politicians to account, an action that deeply affected Jack's life and his family.

As I began documenting Jack's story, drawing on crumbling newspapers and bound minute books - each page, recorded in copperplate handwriting, signed by Jack - the characters jostled one another to leap into life. I needed to loosen my grip on the recorded facts and set these characters free to tell their own story. My role would be to ensure they told their tales truthfully.

Main Players

Jack O'Leary	Organiser South-eastern District ARU 1926 - 1930
John Hayes	Disgraced organiser for South-eastern District ARU
Tim Moroney	State Secretary ARU 1920 - 1944
George Rymer	State President ARU 1921 - 1930
Fred Paterson	ARU supporter and member of CPA
Tom Rickard	Woolloongabba Goods Yards; Unemployed Workers Movement
Frank Ryan	Small-time criminal
Ted Theodore	Queensland Premier 1919 -1925; Deputy Prime Minister & Federal Treasurer 1927 - 1931
Bill McCormack	Queensland Premier 1925 -1929
Joe Collings	State Organiser ALP 1919 - 1931
Forgan Smith	Queensland Premier 1932 -1942
Larcombe	Minister for Railways
Davidson	Commissioner for Railways
ARU	Australian Railways Union
AWU	Australian Workers Union
AFULE	Australian Federated Union of Locomotive Employees
ALP	Australian Labor Party
CPA	Communist Party of Australia

- PART ONE -

There comes a time in the life of every man when he comes up against what he considers to be an injustice so grave that he cannot tolerate it, and he begins to kick. If he is in an organisation, he kicks in an organised way.

Fred Paterson

Chapter 1 - Living on the line (1912-1914)

The hand pumper rattled to a stop at Monkland station: the end of the line. Fluffy white clouds kept pace with the breeze that flapped the chiffon hem around Mary's ankles; blue metal scuffed the cream leather of her shoes as she jumped from the splintered deck. Before her, two iron railway lines gave way to rows of canvas tents that, in the sunlight, looked whiter than they actually were.

Jack lifted the trunk, upon which Mary had sat during the switchback ride out from the township of Gympie, and hoisted it onto his shoulder. Mary O'Leary fidgeted with the gold band on her left hand. She would have to become accustomed to her new name: until yesterday, she had been Mary Stevenson. She fell in beside Jack as he stepped towards the rows of tents.

Inquisitive women lifted their heads and smiled at the newcomer. Men, playing cards in the shade beneath some trees, looked in her direction, assessing Jack's new wife at a glance. Self-consciously, Mary rotated the ring around her finger again.

In her naivety, she had expected to catch a train to the railway camp: her first disappointment as a married woman. Instead, she had perched on her trunk - containing all those things young women collect: tea set, bed linen, towels, table cloths - holding on to her dignity, her skirt and her wide brimmed hat, as the trolley travelled at break-neck speed down the hills. It had been a hair-raising ride, no doubt designed to take the starch out of this young blonde Scottish lass. As Jack and his mate pumped the trolley from Gympie to Monkland, he hid his amusement, knowing this was a learning experience for Mary.

Mary hooked her arm through Jack's. He felt her shudder as she surveyed the scene before her. The families each had two tents, one placed behind the other. In the front tents, curtains separated the children's beds from the parents'; the rear tents, for daily life, were cluttered with boxes and tins around tables draped with limp tablecloths. Jack could see how alien it must have looked to his new wife.

'You'll get used to it love. It's not as bad as it looks.'

The spring air ruffled a wattle shrub, robbing the blossom of its scent as they stopped in front of a tent exactly the same as all the others, except it had a posy of the wattle blossom over the flap, and a sign:

Do not disturb!

Jack set down the trunk and, to Mary's embarrassment, carried her into the tent. What she saw made her heart sink. Two camp stretchers were wired together and beyond them stood a stack of four kerosene boxes, each converted to a drawer by the addition of a wooden cotton reel as a knob, topped by a brown dish festooned with melted tallow.

Mary turned to Jack who was anxiously awaiting her response. She stood on her toes and kissed him. 'You'd better leave me to my unpacking.'

They had arrived on a Sunday, a day of rest for the navvies. With a sense of relief, Jack joined the men under the trees.

The women stoked fires beneath boilers, kneaded dough on trestles in front of their tents, wiped the dirty faces of children who wandered off to make them dirty all over again, chased camp dogs away from food safes. Grey washing flapped between tree trunks.

Mary changed into more suitable clothing and folded her town frock into her trunk. Outside the rear of the tent she flung a linen cloth across a table made out of an old door - still with the hole where the knob had been and supported by thick crossed branches lashed together. Removing the posy from the front tent flap, she took a tin mug from another stack of kerosene boxes - this time stacked as shelves - and scooped water from a large tin covered by a hessian bag. Fresh air flowed through the tent when she lifted the flaps at the front and the rear.

That evening Jack and Mary sat around the campfire listening to rugged men play sensitive airs, jigs and reels on accordions, fiddles and tin whistles. The night was cool and the fire welcome. Children danced until they tired, then curled up on rugs with their heads resting on their mothers' laps.

Mary and Jack retired to their tent which didn't look quite so small by the light of the slush lamp, but when they lay on the crisp new sheets, the ridge between the two stretchers inhibited their embrace. Jack pulled Mary onto his stretcher. The night before - their wedding night - they had shared a double bed, the largest either of them had ever slept in. Now they were cramped onto one camp stretcher.

At the first hint of dawn Jack rose quietly. Mary lifted her head: 'Where are you going?'

'Shh,' he whispered, 'go back to sleep. There's no need for you to wake yet'.

She propped on one elbow.

'But shouldn't I be preparing you breakfast or something?'

'No need. I'll brew up a cuppa and be off.'

When Mary rose, she sat at the table outside the tent and wrote a long letter home, telling her family all about the wedding and how she wished they had been there to see her ivory silk gown. She thought of her father, so dear to her. The last time she had seen him was the first time she had seen him cry. Standing on the platform at Glasgow, with tears running down his cheeks, this dour man knew he would not see his daughter again. He was too old and ill, and Australia was beyond his reach. Mary cursed the betrayal of the young man that had forced her from her home, too embarrassed to face the relatives and friends who had been anticipating their marriage. She also cursed her one-time best friend who now bore his child.

Mary's life changed when she met Jack soon after arriving in her new country. The Botanical Gardens, on the edge of the city, had become a gathering place for young immigrants, and Mary often shared a picnic lunch with two shipboard friends, Emma and John. Jack had worked in the Welsh coal mines with John and when he arrived six weeks after Mary, he joined the young people on the green lawns.

Mary finished her letter and, as she removed her glasses to wipe clean the thick lenses, imagined she saw movement beneath the tent flap. She went inside to investigate, but nothing stirred. In the early afternoon she walked to the on-site store to purchase food for the evening meal. Entering the supply tent, she met a young woman, about her own age, followed by a curly-headed child, face smudged with dirt, chewing its index finger. The woman introduced herself as Alice Johnson. As they talked, Alice expounded on camp life: there were some women, but the camp was mainly made up of men. Mary mentally added isolation to the growing list of disadvantages of living on the line. Drink was all-important to the navvies, explained Alice. This storekeeper sold sly grog and many of the workers brewed their own beer.

'You get to know when to keep out of their way. Paydays are the worst, they get into the beer and start fighting. You'll find it easier to stay indoors when that happens.'

After dark, Jack returned to a table laid with cutlery from Mary's glory-box and the lamp from beside the bed.

'How was your day?' Mary asked in wifely fashion.

'We spent most of it digging rocks from the cutting then barrowing them to the gully. Hard work!' Jack said through a mouthful of mashed potato, pumpkin and corn beef. 'I say, this is a grand meal.'

They punctuated dinner with detailed descriptions of their day.

Later, lying in the crook of Jack's arm in pre-sleep drowsiness, Mary listened to the rustlings of night animals exploring the food box outside the tent.

It did not occur to Jack that his bride would not share his spirit of freedom.

∾

Summer closed in, the heat, the flies, the cockroaches and the mosquitoes became unbearable. Mary was so fair. Her translucent skin burnt bright red as she carried out simple chores such as hanging out washing or walking to the store tent. The rest of the camp, including Jack whose freckled skin had hardened to the sun, refreshed themselves in the waterholes near the camp - the midges seemed to show scarcely any interest in their skin. Mary could only watch from the bank, clothed from head to toe.

Resentfully, Mary settled into the role of camp wife. Using a camp oven she became a proficient baker of bread and damper. The store provided the flour she needed, which she spread in the sun to kill the weevils. She could sift their bodies from the flour. Her days were occupied with reading, preparing food, talking to Alice and watching the bullock teams strain past with their loads of freshly cut logs from further west near Brooloo. Each evening she and Jack sat at their table discussing the day. Safety, an issue that was always on the navvies' minds, dominated their evening talks.

Jack enjoyed working on the railways, found companionship among the fellow navvies who lived together in a village of canvas, but living on the line was also fraught with frustration. He had joined the newly-formed Queensland Railways Union and had become the navvies' 'rep', but he was not a patient man, and felt continually frustrated by the lack of action caused by isolation on the line. It took weeks for grievances to reach the contractor and for decisions to be relayed to the ganger.

Accidents happened.

On Christmas Eve of 1912, just three months after Mary arrived in camp, Jack and two other navvies were working a couple of miles down the line, shoring up a cutting. The three men knew the job was too big for them. They had complained for days but the ganger, under orders to complete the bridge over the Mary River before the arrival of the wet season, could not spare any more men.

The three men were juggling a twelve-foot-long post, straining to keep it upright, when the bottom slipped out and crashed across the thigh of one of the men. His bone shattered with a sickening crunch. Jack and the other man froze for a few seconds before jemmying the log from the smashed leg. They threaded the arms of Jack's jacket through two saplings and ran back along the gravel bed to the pumper at the railhead with the wounded man jiggling between them on the makeshift stretcher, and lay him on the pumper and started off down the line for Gympie and medical help. Miraculously, the doctor saved his leg, but it had been a close call.

&

As the line crept further from Monkland, it became impractical for the men to return to camp each evening and trek back to the worksite the following morning. Every few weeks they loaded drays with their tents, furniture and clothes, to be pulled by draughthorses a couple of miles down the track. A temporary grocery store followed. When they needed to find another site, the process started all over again. Again and again.

Creating a garden in which to grow herbs and vegetables was impossible under such conditions, but the resourceful camp women adapted by using old kerosene tins with holes punched in the bottom. Fruiting tomato plants rode atop the drays with the rest of the camping gear. Mary had her share of potted herbs, mostly parsley, marjoram and thyme. The thyme masked the gamey flavour of the rabbits she purchased from the rabbit-trapper who called by the camp.

~

On a Monday in January 1913 the rain started: rain like Mary had never seen. Unlike the drizzle of Scotland, it turned the red dirt into mud that stuck to everything. By lunchtime, muddy water had found its way beneath the canvas walls. Using a spade, Mary dug a channel around the perimeter of the tent and the puddles on the floor reduced in size. Then the trenches overflowed. The water seeped up the sides of the kerosene boxes, saturating their clothes and leaving her trunk in three inches of water.

Already wet through from perspiration, Mary foraged in the rain for rocks, branches, anything she could use to lift their possessions out of the slush. Her hair stuck to her face as she spent the rest of the day rearranging their home. When she had finished, she sat on the bed and cried before changing into dry clothes.

Jack ended the day covered with mud from head to foot and his hair clamped to his scalp. Mary held out a towel and clean clothes and pointed him in the direction of the camp shower. He returned clean enough for Mary to see his face again.

'How long will this last?' Mary was desperate.

'Probably about a week, although I've seen it go on for longer.'

They sat side by side on the stretcher: Mary exhausted and dispirited; Jack trying to pacify her.

'Surely you won't work in this?' Mary dreaded the thought of being imprisoned in the tent alone, day after day.

'Construction doesn't stop because of rain, Mary, it just means we shovel mud instead of dirt.'

But Mary wasn't listening to Jack. She sat, paralysed with fear as a black snake emerged from beneath her trunk and slithered across the muddy floor towards the bed. Her scream jammed in her throat.

Jack followed her stare.

'Oh shit! Stay on the bed!'

He grabbed the shovel and plunged it into the tough, rubbery body just below the head with such force that a third of the blade disappeared into the earth, taking the head with it. The headless snake continued to writhe, exposing a scarlet belly.

Mary found her scream.

৵

The rain poured relentlessly for the next week, and the navvies had no choice but to cease work. It became impossible to light a fire, to wash, to dry clothes. Each morning, Mary checked her musty boots for intruders seeking refuge from the wet (sometimes finding scorpions, at other times, spiders) before pulling them over her wrinkled feet that itched as the skin began to peel from her soles.

By the following Saturday the rain had eased a little and patches of blue appeared in the western sky. Of course, with the sun came the dreadful humidity that sapped her energy and laboured her breathing, and a new generation of mosquitoes and midges swarmed and attacked. Mary thought the torture would never end.

The wet season had arrived, and with it typhoid, dysentery and diphtheria visited the young children of the camp. Once a week a doctor travelled the line from Gympie. He made diagnoses and returned with medication the following week.

Alice's little girl enjoyed splashing with the other naked children in the mud, until diphtheria swelled her tongue and threatened to block her windpipe. Alice spent weeks in Gympie before she could bring her daughter back to camp. The mothers of the well children lived on a knife-edge, trying to keep them out of the mud and away from the ill children, shooing flies from their food, slapping at the mosquitoes that sucked their blood. They collected rainwater for drinking, hoping it wasn't contaminated. They suspected the illness came from the pit toilets that filled with rain, spreading their contents over the earth where the children played.

The canvas walls didn't afford any privacy as illness continued throughout the winter. Mary lay awake listening to muffled sounds of lovemaking and the cries of children as their mothers, weary from their own colds and influenza, crooned them back to sleep.

By August, although the bridge across the Mary River still wasn't finished, a loco pulling one carriage was able to slowly make its way to the far side of the river carrying councillors and businessmen from Gympie. With much pomp and ceremony, they enjoyed a picnic on the riverbank while the men toiled below and the women worked at turning the pitiful camps into homes.

Letters from home were infrequent. They always brought news, but sometimes the news was very sad. Mary learned of the death of her baby sister Polly - whom she had never met - boiled beneath an upturned pot of water; and her larrikin brother Archie, trampled by a draughthorse when a prank misfired. He was just seven. Mary placed the letters in her trunk, along with another telling of the death of her father, and grieved alone.

February 1914 steamed its way in, and Mary awoke one morning feeling queasy. Jack was alarmed at the paleness of her cheeks. He lit the kerosene stove to boil the billy, but the smell made her vomit. Jack sat on the edge of the stretcher, stroking her hair from her clammy forehead: 'I think we'd better get the doctor to take a look at you when he comes through next week'.

He dressed for work in the pre-dawn grey and reluctantly left Mary with an enamelled basin beside the bed, saying: 'I'll ask Alice to keep an ear open for you'.

When he returned that evening, Mary was up and about, feeling on top of the world, with dinner prepared. Jack's relief was obvious.

Next day brought the same routine, and the next until Jack realised what Mary suspected all along. He asked her straight: 'So, wife of mine, are we going to have a child?'

'It looks that way. I've had my suspicions for a few weeks now. I wasn't sure if you'd like the idea.'

'It was bound to happen some time.'

Mary had hoped for a more enthusiastic response.

To Mary, the rain, the heat, the insects, the crawling creatures, the cold, the discomfort, the loneliness now seemed secondary. However, there was something she needed to discuss with Jack: she had seen the other families striving to lead normal lives on the line, had seen their children fall ill. She had watched these children go off to the local school and heard tales of how the resident children taunted the 'camp children'. Mary did not wish this child of hers to live that kind of life. She asked Jack to consider leaving the line. He grew quiet, speaking only when spoken to. Mary knew she had offended him.

He said he would think about it.

However, there was another birth to celebrate before that of Jack and Mary's baby. On 13 February 1914 the first train ran on the Mary Valley Line: halfway, as far as Kandanga. A gang, including Jack, was still at work metalling the yards when the train arrived an hour and forty minutes after leaving Gympie. Horse-drawn vehicles lined up waiting for their deliveries, and many excited people crowded onto the platform. For the first time, Mary was able to appreciate the major contribution people like Jack were making to life in rural Australia. She could see a purpose for being there, and perhaps such terrible living conditions would soon end.

It was another two weeks before the official opening of the line took place amidst much fanfare. Important citizens were invited: the Minister for Railways, Mr Paget; Sir William McGregor; Mr Walker MLA and of course, their wives.

The organisers did not consider the injustice of inviting dignitaries to a free banquet while asking the three hundred workers and their families to pay 7/6d each to attend. Nor did it occur to most of the workers to question this injustice.

The official train, draped with flags and foliage and bearing the State's coat of arms, stopped just short of the station to allow McGregor, Paget and Walker to mount the footplate and drive the train to the platform, breaking through the ribbon held on either side of the track by their wives. Everyone cheered and detonators exploded, all in the liquid mud and heavy rain that would not stop.

Ladies in their finest garments slithered through the quagmire, holding up ankle-length skirts with one hand and small, impractically fussy umbrellas with the other.

Not far from the railway station stood a building, complete except for interior walls, which the owner, Mr Boyling, had offered for the banquet. It was no coincidence that he was in the process of applying for a licence to operate a hotel. His kindly donation would not go unnoticed by those who held his future in their hands.

As the last of the officials made their way into the building, a driver of a cream cart came down the street at top speed, throwing mud over the parliamentarians and railway magnates.

With a smile, Jack took Mary's arm and turned her away from the town to return to their sodden camp.

∂

Mary was now four months pregnant and they still had not discussed leaving the line. One evening, as they ate yet another pot of rabbit stew and dumplings, Mary told Jack he had to make up his mind to leave within the next few weeks.

'But I like the railways, Mary. I've been at it for three years now. I know most of the workers - I'm one of them. I don't know any other work, except for mining, and there's no-one could make me go back to that.'

Mary fired off questions in quick succession: 'What happens when this line's finished? Are we to move on to the next camp, and the next? Do you want your child to grow up being looked down upon? How are we to educate him?'

'An education isn't everything, Mary. Other families live on the line, and they aren't people I would look down on.'

'Maybe not, but people who live in the towns do. And if you must know, I miss living in town. Be honest, you do too!'

'Actually, I like the freedom of living in the camp. I can walk for hours without meeting another person. How could I do that in a town?'

Mary rose from the table and walked into the tent, fearing she was losing the argument. Lying on the bed, she cried quietly, although not so quietly that Jack couldn't hear.

Jack recognised the fierce determination concentrated in Mary's compact body. He weighed this up together with the fact that, in a matter of months, the Melawondi Tunnel would be cemented and with that, the earthworks finished. Most of his workmates, paid off, would head to the next construction site.

He followed Mary into the tent and sat beside her.

'Okay love, I'll see what I can arrange. I'll probably be able to get work at the Ipswich Workshops.'

They lay together, lost in their own thoughts: Mary's full of hope for a better future; Jack's full of sadness for the life he was being forced to leave so near the end of the job. However, he also realised that gaining wider experience in the railway business would make him a more effective union representative.

A fortnight later, Jack and Mary spent the morning loading their meagre possessions onto a dray for the final time. Jack dismantled the camp table, tossed the legs into the wood-heap, and leant the old door against a tree. Perhaps it would be useful to someone else. Mary packed the crockery and cooking utensils she had accumulated from a Gympie hawker into large wooden cases.

As Jack stowed his work-worn clothes into the battered old case he had lifted onto his shoulders four years before when he stepped off the gangplank from the *Kaipara* onto the sunny wharf in Brisbane, he reflected on his life. Having floated from school to the coal mines in Wales at twelve, from coal mines to the merchant navy at sixteen, he had then packed his trunk - with no more preparation than it takes to leave on vacation - and left for the far side of the world at twenty-three. Mary longingly stroked her city clothes, and added her plain gaberdine bush clothes to her case.

All morning they worked side by side, each in their own world. Mary was oblivious to Jack's sadness: each part of their humble home had been of his own making, and each neighbour made up his world. And then there were the mountains on either side that framed his view to the coast.

After lunch, Jack walked in the bush one last time, through the brush boxes, the black wattles, the eucalypts, the paper barks - all familiar to him. He ran his hand across the soft seed heads of the kangaroo grass, walked along the richly rain-forested gully, sat on a large rock and stared into the bubbling stream where a catfish fanned its pebbly nest.

Mary waited on her trunk in the centre of a 6ft by 6ft patch of bare earth and her anticipation faded to disquiet. Until now, they had not led a normal married life. They shared a bed and the evening meal, the rest of Jack's day consisted solely of railwaymen and union business. Mary thought of the years stretched ahead, perhaps more than this one child. How would Jack adjust to living with a family, in a house? Would he cope with the call of fatherhood?

࿄

Jack handed Mary the front door key. 'Here, I think you should be the one to open it.'

She felt the solid clunk as it turned in the lock. Mary walked through the hallway that split the cottage - a bedroom on either side and a lounge opposite the kitchen - into the back yard. Past the clothes' line stood a toilet, complete with a wooden seat and pan. She could not hide her delight.

'Why so much excitement over a toilet? We had one at the camp.'

Mary remembered balancing on a sapling over a ditch in the drizzling rain and replied: 'Surely you can't compare that with this!'

'I can't see anything wrong with what we had. It served perfectly well.'

The following Monday Mary waved Jack off to work and walked through the house stroking her swelling stomach. She took her time attending to the household chores - emptying the ash drawer to the stove, restocking the kindling box - revelling in the normality that she had missed for the past eighteen months.

At each intersection Jack was joined by other riders tossing hellos back and forth, all heading for the same place. To Jack, the scale of the Ipswich Workshops was truly impressive: craft shops, a powerhouse with its own coalmine, a canteen and a steam mill sprawled across a hundred acres and, by the river, tents for the migrant workers were erected amongst vegetable gardens and flowers. Two rows of red brick sheds stood sentinel over the transverser lines that delivered locos and carriages through their arched doorways. At lunchtime, Jack sat in front of a rostrum outside the canteen and listened to the spruikers.

ॐ

Jack and Mary settled well into life in Liverpool Street. The workers had formed a choir and an informal sports club. Cricket, tennis, boxing: Jack took part in all the activities. As winter blew into Ipswich, Mary kept the stove burning and adapted her camp cooking. The novelty of the toilet in the back yard wore thin as the nights grew colder and her bladder weaker.

ॐ

Chapter 2 - At war (1914-1919)

On 28 June 1914 a Bosnian student revolutionary named Gavrillo Princip shot Archduke Franz Ferdinand in Sarajevo. Germany declared war on Russia on 1 August. In Ipswich, people flocked to the town centre to talk, to ask questions, to discuss late into the evening. There was something of an air of celebration: the world had anticipated war for months, and many young men - and some young women - found excitement in the prospect of going to battle.

Mary saw the wanderlust stir in Jack as, day after day, his fellow workers left the Workshops to travel to France. She begged him not to leave her, and he agreed he would not, but as news filtered back from Europe of adventures and mishaps, pressure grew on the young, fit men who remained at home. Then, on a crisp spring morning, Mary's first baby, John Alexander, was born into the capable hands of Maude Matthews, midwife.

Jack waited six months before collecting his enlistment papers from the Ipswich Town Hall. That evening, he strode into the kitchen and spread the papers on the table. Mary paused, a spoonful of mashed banana halfway towards Jackie's open mouth.

'What's that?'

'I'm joining up.'

Jack steeled himself for the outburst that would surely ensue. Instead, without a word, Mary collected Jackie from the highchair and whipped the papers from the kitchen table. Walking down the back stairs, she crossed the yard to the incinerator, still smouldering from the day's burning-off, and dropped the papers. She waited for them to catch alight before returning to the house.

'We'll have no more talk of war!'

Angry, insulted, Jack stormed out the front door, mounted his pushbike and headed for the pub. A few hours later he wobbled through the front gate, dismounted and entered the darkened house. Mary feigned sleep as he bumped along the hallway. She heard him look in on Jackie, and through their bedroom wall, heard his loud whisper: 'Don't think you can do what you want when you grow up, little man, because you can't'.

Jack probed his way into their bedroom.

'It's your loving husband returned from the war!'

He collapsed, fully clothed, on the centre of the bed and began to snore. Mary quietly left the bed and curled up on the lounge, but she could not sleep, aware of every movement from the bedroom as Jack fought the sheets through his dream-filled night. When Jack awoke the next day, half of it had already passed. A dry tongue filled his mouth as he wandered the empty house searching for Mary, vaguely aware he should apologise. He found her in the backyard prodding nappies in the copper, baby on hip. Jack sat on the top step, elbows resting on his knees, head down.

'I don't feel too well.'

Mary jabbed at the ballooning nappies.

'I suppose I should apologise.'

Mary placed Jackie in a playpen beneath the mango tree and added a handful of split wood to the fire beneath the copper.

'Only if you mean it.'

'I'm not sorry I tried to sign up, but I am sorry I got drunk.'

'Why do you want to leave us?' Mary's voice emerged shaky, defying attempts to keep it level.

'Oh, Mary, it's not that I want to leave you and Jackie. But just about everyone I know's gone to France.'

She lifted the steaming nappies and dropped them into a tub on the ground, then added another load to the copper.

'If you must go, at least wait until Jackie's had his birthday.'

~

September came, and Jack and Mary helped Jackie blow out the single candle on his birthday cake. A week later, Jack re-entered the town hall and enlisted with the AIF. He reported to the Ipswich Workshops, was granted leave without pay for the duration of the war, then went home and told Mary.

Mary had been keeping a secret the past two months, but her pregnancy merely delayed Jack's departure. Madge was born the week before Jack threw his kitbag onto a train destined for Sydney and his company. Mary returned to their home from the railway station feeling very alone.

~

Mary awoke one morning to a fully-formed thought. She dressed her two small children and travelled by train to Brisbane and the shipping office. Yes, there were berths available for Scotland. In fact, a ship was leaving the next week. Mary went to the bank and, withdrawing the small amount of money she'd been saving, decided this was indeed a rainy day. In a whirlwind of activity, she packed all their clothes into two trunks, hers and the children's in one, Jack's in another, and filled her glory-box with household items she held dear, then arranged for a cart to take them to the wharf on the day of sailing.

However a telegram delivery boy came to her door the day before they were due to leave.

```
All shipping cancelled stop
Call at shipping office stop
```

Her spirits were at their lowest ebb as she renewed the lease on the house in Liverpool Street.

❧

France, 1917, and C Company of the Australian Military Forces - newly arrived to relieve soldiers bogged for months in the mud at Messines - froze beneath 25 degrees of frost.

Side by side, their feet buried in the freezing mud, Jack and a young padre debated whether soldiers got frostbite and whether there was a God as they listened to the Huns blowing their noses and talking to each other. Except for their German words, they sounded the same as the men in Jack's trench. Cigarette packets flew backwards and forwards across no-man's-land in an unlikely trade between workers at either end of the rifles. They yelled 'thanks' or 'danken' to each other, then were chastised by their superiors for fraternising.

Jack returned to reality when a German came over the top and thrust a bayonet at his head. A well-timed shot from an Aussie stopped the steel spike just as it ruptured Jack's eardrum. For a moment, Jack wondered if there might be a God after all.

He lay recuperating for weeks on a stretcher in a French chateau overlooking a garden that glistened with fresh snow, but not a bird sang in the leafless forest beyond. The locals said the birds would return in the spring; at least, they hoped they would. As Jack made leather boots in England for soldiers in France, he questioned whether the world would ever return to normal. His continual requests to return to his company at the Front were denied. On 8

August he took matters into his own hands and, collecting a towel, hair brush, razor and shaving brush, stowed them in the pockets of his greatcoat, and walked out of No. 11 camp at Durrington in London while the rest of C Company assembled for Tattoo.

He had been AWL several times before - most of the soldiers had, it was their way of relieving both boredom and stress - but this time, Jack was leaving for good.

&

Australia was abuzz with discussion over a forthcoming referendum against compulsory conscription. There were many meetings both for and against: those representing Prime Minister Hughes used their considerable strength to quash any demonstration against the Yes vote.

In the small Queensland town of Ipswich, Mary thought hard and long over how she would vote. There was no doubt in her mind what Jack would do - he fervently opposed compulsory military service - however she needed to be sure that her vote reflected how she truly felt. Her husband had chosen to go to war: a choice he had been free to make. Others had gone, not because they chose to do so, but because they could no longer withstand the pressures exerted on them by their community.

Mary attended anti-conscription rallies, heard the words: 'Forcing a man to fight is the same as forcing a woman to fondle; both are vilely outraged. You can't order someone to hate any more than you can order someone to love', and reached her decision. She joined the majority of Australians in voting No to compulsory conscription.

Mary had kept a daily vigil on the mailbox and read Jack's news that was always six weeks old. He skited how he and some of the other soldiers had left camp for a few free days in London. They managed to stay away for a whole week one time before the Military Police found them, boisterously carousing in a hotel, and frogmarched them back to camp. Jack had forfeited three weeks' pay for his adventure.

Mary worked hard to maintain a degree of normality in her life, but grew tired of questions she could not answer:

'Where's Daddy?'

'Can't Daddy tuck me in tonight?'

'Why doesn't Daddy love us?'

'I hate Daddy!'

Money wasn't a problem to start with: three-fifths of Jack's allotment went straight to her, two-fifths to him. Mary developed a good relationship with Mr Rollston, the local grocer and postmaster, and visited his shop at the end of her street almost daily. If Jack's allotment was late, Mr Rollston allowed her to complete her shopping and settle the bill when the money arrived.

Winter drew to a close and, as the spring warmed the little home, Jack's letters ceased. At first Mary suspected a problem with the mail but as weeks turned into months she grew frantic with worry. December came, and she did not receive her allotment.

'No matter, Mrs O'Leary,' said Mr Rollston. 'I know you're good for it. You do your shopping and I'll wait till you get paid. It won't be long, I'm sure.'

The postman stopped by in mid-December, and placed an official envelope in Mary's mailbox.

Dear Mrs. O'Leary,

Your husband, John Laurence O'Leary, has been absent without leave from Durrington Camp, London, since early August. A Court of Enquiry held at Durrington on 28 August declared him an illegal absentee.

There is no option but to suspend your allowance until he returns voluntarily or is apprehended.

Should you know of his whereabouts, we would appreciate your contacting us, and also persuading your husband to return to his unit.

Yours faithfully,

Major Smythe,

Officer In Charge.

A proud and private person by nature, Mary could not accept her status as the wife of a deserter. She needed to maintain her dignity, needed to eat, and yet she had no income and her limited gardening skills were by no means adequate to feed her family. She drew on the small amount of money that would have taken her back to Scotland to pay the rent.

For two weeks she remained inside the house behind drawn curtains; Jackie couldn't understand why they no longer went on daily strolls. One day, as Mary sat in the darkened lounge room, she heard the clatter of hooves on the front path. It gave her quite a start.

'Mrs O'Leary?'

She pretended she wasn't home.

'Mrs O'Leary! Are you in?'

Jackie, rising from his afternoon nap, pulled the bedroom curtains aside and looked from his window.

'It's Mr Rollston,' he called to his mother.

Her cover blown, she opened the door.

Mr Rollston dismounted, raised his hat in greeting and enquired, in a kindly manner: 'Is everything all right, Mrs O'Leary? We haven't seen you for some time.'

'You'd better come in,' she said, leaving the door open for him to follow.

Mr Rollston tethered his horse to the verandah post and followed her into the kitchen. He was a tall man who walked with the stoop of one perpetually on guard against low objects.

'Please, take a seat Mr Rollston.'

'Thank you, Mrs O'Leary.' He folded his lean body onto a chair but Mary remained standing.

'Mrs Rollston and I are worried about you and your bairns. Is there anything we can do to help?'

Some people command respect because of their integrity, and Mr Rollston was such a man. During the three and a half years Mary had known him, she had never once heard him discuss anyone else's business. She had to trust someone, still, the words stuck in her throat as she prepared to take her grocer into her confidence.

'I can see you're distressed. What's happened? Is Mr O'Leary well?'

'They've stopped my allowance.'

'If it's food you're worrying about, we'll stand by you. I know you're an honest woman.'

'Thank you,' she said with sincere gratitude.

He remained seated, encouraging her to make a further explanation.

Mary removed an envelope from the dresser drawer and handed it to him. He read the enclosed letter from the officer-in-charge.

'Oh goodness me, what a predicament. Have you not heard from Jack?'

'Not a word for over five months. I don't even know if he's alive.'

'Well, my dear, all we can do is wait for news.'

He rose.

'In the meantime, Mrs Rollston and I are only too pleased to assist in any way we can.'

As Mary thanked the kindly man, she wondered how many other needy people he was 'assisting'.

❧

Christmas came and went. When people enquired after Jack, Mary replied: 'Oh, he's waiting to rejoin his mates in France. He was injured in combat, you know. A German bayoneted him in his ear. He's lucky to be alive!'

On New Year's Day she awoke and said, 'Happy birthday Jack, wherever you are'.

The following day, as Mary weeded the small herb garden by the front stairs, the postman stopped at her fence. He blew his shrill whistle, and waved an envelope.

'A letter, Mrs O'Leary. It's been a while, hasn't it?'

He smiled as he tipped his cap and handed her the envelope then peddled off, straight-backed, down the road.

Her fingers left garden-soil prints on the envelope as, with shaking hands, she broke the seal and unfolded a single sheet of blank paper wrapped around five English pound notes.

〜

The transport ship *Boravia* pitched her way through the icy black channel from France to England in the early hours of 20th March 1918, oblivious of the German torpedo whizzing towards her stern. John O'Brien slept fitfully during the crossing. At 5am all hell broke loose. John woke as his hammock, swinging violently, catapulted him across the deck. Within minutes, the only trace that the *Boravia* had ever existed was burning debris floating on oily waves.

Keenly aware that he needed to ration his last salty breath, John untangled his legs from cloth and ropes that dragged him beneath the muck on the waves. He struck out with his arms, not entirely sure which way was up. His probing fingers found two recesses that felt like eye sockets. He heard bubbles rising beside him and followed them. With lungs fit to burst, he pushed through hard timber and soft bodies, hoping, with each passing moment, to waken from this dream. He broke the surface into a black world as his lungs began to suck in the evil-smelling salty water.

Daylight turned the black night to dark grey. John floated amongst unrecognisable pieces of ship, swallowing the freezing bitter water as waves lifted and dumped him amongst other floating men, mostly dead. He swam towards a hatchway flung from the ship when the torpedo had struck, and dragged the top half of his body onto its splintered timbers where he drifted in and out of consciousness.

Hands grabbed at his bony shoulders, lost grip, found his arms. Delirious, he shouted up to his rescuers: 'My name's John O'Brien!'

As the crew of the hospital ship hauled the lean freckled body on deck, they said: 'Okay John. We've got you'.

~

Margaret Gibson was preparing the evening meal in her home in Glasgow when she heard a knock at the front door. She opened it to a lanky stranger, his auburn hair soaked by drizzling rain and his fists stuffed into the pockets of a greatcoat.

'Mrs Gibson? You've never met me. I'm married to your sister Mary. I'm Jack O'Leary.'

'John!' Margaret called into her house. She turned to the stranger: 'You'd better come in'.

John Gibson appeared in the hallway, newspaper in one hand, pipe bowl in the other, warm carpet slippers on his feet, and a query on his ruddy face.

'This here's our Mary's Jack,' Margaret said, removing her apron and smoothing her fair hair that curled beneath her ears. Jack would have taken her for Mary's sister even if he hadn't known who she was. The same diminutive figure, upturned nose, even the slight turn in her right eye. Margaret removed Jack's woollen coat from his shoulders and shook the rain from it, releasing its musty smell, while John steered Jack towards the lounge room and a crackling fire.

'Hoot mon. What brings you here in this condition?'

Jack towelled his hair into a tangled mop and accepted a tumbler of scotch from his brother-in-law. He waited for the warmth to fill his stomach, and Margaret to join them, before answering.

'Firstly, I want you both to call me John O'Brien. I'm on the run from the MPs, have been for the past seven months. O'Brien's my mother's maiden name,' he explained. 'I copped a bayonet in the ear and they wouldn't let me go back to France - there's some stupid rule that says I'm only good for making boots in England - so I left camp. I made my way to Ireland and joined the navy, but my boat was torpedoed and I swallowed half the English Channel. I've spent the past few months in hospital with pneumonia.' He tapped his chest. 'It's left me with a cough.'

'So why have you come to Scotland?' asked John.

Jack turned to Margaret: 'Mary's told me that you work in a munitions factory. I thought you might be able to get me some work there'.

Margaret nodded. 'They are short handed; but wouldn't it make more sense to go back to the navy?'

'They've started asking questions and I suspect they've guessed I'm not who I say I am, so I thought it best to get out. I know it's a lot to ask, but could I stay here for a while?'

'No problem there. Does Mary know where you are?' asked Margaret.

'No. I can't tell her in case her mail's censored. I send her a bit of money whenever there's some spare, so she knows I'm still kicking.'

When Jack was fed and bedded, Margaret took a notepad and pen and wrote to her sister in Australia.

Initially, Jack kept a low profile at the factory, but when munitions workers across Glasgow went on strike in an attempt to secure the release of a leading Scottish socialist, John MacLean, who had been imprisoned for sedition two years before, he found himself caught up in political activity. It shook Jack out of his hibernation and caused him to consider the futility of being hunted around Britain while his own union and family battled on in Australia. Therefore it came as a relief when, a few months later, loud repetitive knocking disturbed the Gibson household at two o'clock one morning. John raced down the stairs tying his dressing gown cord, opened the front door, and was pushed aside by a constable from the Glasgow Police: 'I've reason to believe John Laurence O'Leary is in this house'.

John stood aside and waved his hand in the direction of the stairs he'd just descended. As the constable took the stairs two at a time, a tousled head appeared through a bedroom door.

'I think it's me you're after.'

'Are you John Laurence O'Leary, and are you an absentee from the 36th Battalion of the Australian Infantry Forces?'

'Guess there's no use denying it.'

When a young Private from the Garrison Military Police in Brisbane arrived in Ipswich to interview a young wife in the hope of locating a missing soldier, he was unaware that the subject of his investigation was being held at Lewes Detention Barracks awaiting court-martial - such was the delayed state of communication between England and Australia during the war.

Mary opened her door, surprised to see a man in uniform standing to attention, his cap under his left arm.

'Mrs O'Leary?'

'Yes?'

'Private Svenson from the Military Police. May I come in?'

Mary led him to the lounge room and, with the wave of her hand invited him to sit. But he remained standing, ill at ease, disliking the job on which he had been sent.

'As you know Mrs O'Leary, your husband has been absent without leave from his unit at Durrington Camp for twelve months. We'd really like to draw this matter to a close, and we feel you may be able to shed some light on his whereabouts.'

'I've no idea where he is. If I did I'd tell you, believe me. I'm stuck here with no allotment and two kids to feed.'

'So you've absolutely no ideas?'

Mary, never a convincing liar, felt her cheeks flush.

'What'll happen to Jack when he's found?'

'He'll have to face a court-martial, then he'll be sentenced.'

'What will happen to him after that?'

'He'll most likely be placed in detention. I can't say for how long, although it would be a minimum of two years.'

At least he paid her the courtesy of allowing a few minutes silence while she weighed up the consequences. Mary walked to the open window where she watched Madge and Jackie playing in the yard. They deserved to have a father. If she didn't help the Military Police he could be on the run for years; if she did assist, they would not see him for another two years.

She turned to face the young private waiting patiently for her reply.

'He's in Scotland, in Glasgow, working in a munitions factory. I can't tell you more than that. Now I wish you good day, sir.'

'Please contact us if you hear anything further. Good day, Mrs O'Leary.'

He pulled the front door behind him and replaced his cap, feeling pity for the young woman left inside.

Throughout the day, Mary fought a battle between her conscience and her sense of duty. Late in the afternoon she wrote:

August 23rd 1918

To The Officer in Charge,

Sir,

I had a visit from one of the Military Police today, asking the whereabouts of my husband, (J.L. O'Leary). I gave him what information I could, but have since been thinking the matter over.

I want to state that my sister knows where he is, according to the latest letter from her. My sister's name is Mrs. John Gibson, 2 Malvern Place, off Bomely Park St, East Glasgow.

I hope you will be able to find him, it is not that I wish him to be punished, but I am left in very straightened circumstances, and I have two little children to keep.
Trusting this will suit you, I remain
Yours faithfully
M.H. O'Leary.
Ps. Would you kindly let me know the result of your inquiries as soon as possible?

Before Mary had time to rethink her actions, she sealed the envelope, changed into street clothes and walked the children to Mr Rollston's store. A bell tinkled above the shop door as Mary pushed it open. She cursed silently as she recognised a neighbour being served at the counter. Mary nodded her greeting and handed the envelope to Mr Rollston who, upon studying the address, raised a querying eyebrow to her. Mary bowed her head ever so slightly. Her neighbour, pretending to read the instructions on a soap packet, curiously watched the exchange. Mr Rollston stamped the envelope and added it to the sack for delivery.

Mary returned home and sat in the dark, already regretting her actions.

On 13 September, Mary was informed that the Officer-in-Charge of the AIF 'had pleasure' in resuming her allotment.

❧

Late in the afternoon of 11th November every church bell in Ipswich peeled without stop. Jackie hung over the front fence watching the procession of people on foot, in horse and cart and on bicycle, heading to the town centre, joyously celebrating the end of the war. Mary was not yet ready to celebrate. She still had no idea of the whereabouts of her husband, or what was to be his fate. However, as the excitement reached fever pitch, she felt obliged to join in, if only for her children who needed to share in this communal relief.

Her next-door neighbour, hitching his pony to his cart, called to Jackie: 'Tell your mother she's welcome to ride to town with us'.

Jackie ran inside and pleaded with his mother.

As Mary sat beside the Johnsons with her two-and-a-half year-old daughter on her knee and her very grown up four year-old son next to her, Mr Johnson said: 'Looks like our boys have lost their jobs, eh?'

Mary had no idea so many people lived in Ipswich: flags flew; bands played; people danced, sang and laughed. There were fireworks. The desperation and loneliness Mary had felt for the past year retreated for a few hours as the crowd drew her into their joy.

At seven o'clock Mr Johnson suggested they should be heading home with her weary bairns. When Mary had put Jackie and Madge to bed, she sat on the back steps. 'Jack, where the hell are you?'

≈

Having been found guilty of desertion before a court-martial, Jack was in Lewes Detention Barracks preparing to serve two years' imprisonment. He had a good counsel who pointed out that his AWL was not in order to avoid military service; on the contrary, it had been an attempt to serve in an even higher degree and capacity since, frustrated by seven months of being refused a return to France, Jack had deserted in order to join the Royal Navy. Counsel produced letters of support from the captain of Jack's ship and from the manager of the National Projectile Factory in Glasgow. He begged for mercy on Jack's behalf. On 15 November Counsel visited Jack's cell with the news that the rest of his term had been remitted and he was to return to his training barracks.

≈

Mary and the children were sitting at their meal one evening in early April 1919 when, without fuss or ceremony, Jack walked along the hallway and back into their lives. Mary looked up from her plate. 'Oh, my God!' Turning to the children staring at the stranger before them, she said: 'Madge and Jackie, it's your father'.

Smell is important; each person has an individual odour. Jack smelt different. As they lay in bed that evening, Mary felt she was lying beside a stranger. Patiently, Jack began to court her all over again.

≈

Chapter 3 - Restless (1919-1924)

As with all the soldiers, Jack had returned to his family a changed man. A mature determination tempered his carefree enthusiasm. He would not discuss the war with Mary. It belonged to the past. Best forgotten.

He felt like a stranger living in a house that was a home to his wife and children. The space he had once occupied in the family no longer existed. It had been taken over by a little girl with a pale face and blonde hair - and this little girl did not know who he was.

Jackie was proud of his father: a soldier, returned from the Big War. He used a stick to play 'rifles', bayoneted trees: 'Cop that, ya Hun!'

When Jack saw this, he grabbed the stick, broke it over his knee, and sent Jackie to his bedroom.

'What do you expect?' Mary snapped at Jack. 'All he hears is talk of how the brave soldiers have freed us.'

'There will be no war propaganda in this house!'

Jackie came out of his bedroom and began kicking his father in the shins and punching him in the stomach, tears running down his dirty little face: 'I hate you! I hate you! Why did you come home!' and ran back to his room, slamming his door and leaving Jack and Mary stunned.

Returning to the Ipswich Railway Workshops was far less traumatic than returning to his home. Jack slipped back into his old position amongst mates who had shared the same experiences. They had no need to speak of the war and the terrible scars, visible and invisible, they bore.

Jack took the British War Medal the government sent him and tossed it into a box containing his uniform, kitbag and various letters. He had no use for it. He consigned the box to the darkness at the bottom of his wardrobe. He did, however, have use for the £3 pension allocated for his deafness.

Despite Jack's reluctance to remember or even discuss the war, it was with pride that he led Mary and the children the couple of miles to the Workshops one Saturday in September. Many railway workers had enlisted, some hadn't returned. Each worker who had remained on the job at the Workshops during the war contributed 1% of his pay to build the only private cenotaph in Australia.

Extra trains travelled to Ipswich from Brisbane and everyone dressed in their best clothes. Dignitaries were invited to take part in the procession and were plied with afternoon tea while the workers who had paid for the memorial, along with those whose names appeared on its plaques, were charged sixpence each to take afternoon tea in the canteen. Echoes of the opening of the Mary Valley railway line.

The Blackstone-Ipswich Cambrian Choir and the Ipswich Model Band performed on the grass, and a pipe band led the procession. The pipes stirred the souls of most people who were present. For Mary, Scottish born and bred and a long way from home and family, their effect was profound.

The Workshop employees had every reason to feel proud of the monument: thirty-two feet of Victorian granite, topped by a seven-foot bronze soldier shipped all the way from London. The Governor unveiled the plaques, everyone crowded around, this was what they'd come to see. Men peered intently at the list of names and turned, grinning, to their families to point to their names. A few women stood alone, found the names they sought, and drifted away.

Jack lifted Madge onto his shoulder, and pointed out his name in the middle of the front plaque.

Arriving home, Mary said, in a mood contrary to Jack's: 'What a pleasant afternoon'.

'I dunno, it brings it all back,' Jack said.

As Mary unlocked the door, he collected his pushbike and wheeled from the verandah. 'I need to go out again.'

Mary shepherded Jackie and Madge into the hallway, knowing Jack would find some mates who also needed to drown their memories.

⁂

At times, employees from the Ipswich Workshops were brought before the Appeals Board to question decisions that affected their lives. Many found this an intimidating experience and, permitted to choose a union delegate to put their case, selected Jack who had a talent for such representations.

In order to gain first-hand experience to better argue these cases, Jack worked in all the sheds within the Ipswich Workshops: the boiler shop; erecting shop; machine shop; wagon shop; carriage shop; wheel shop; wood-working shop; sawmills; breaking-down room; stores and roundhouse.

By the end of 1919 he felt he must transfer to other workshops if he was to further his union work. And so began a four-year stint of house moving.

A week after arriving in Rockhampton, Jack was in Brisbane before the Appeals Board representing Mick Hanson, a lad of seventeen dismissed after an accident involving another lad of eighteen.

Jack argued that the accident was a result of the Commissioner's propensity to cut corners: getting cleaners - who were only boys - to act as firemen, and young firemen to drive the locos within the shunting yards, thus saving on wages.

Of course the lads loved it, it made them feel like men, but they lacked the experience to cope with emergencies.

On the evening in question, Mick shunted an engine to the loco shed for an overhaul with his mate, Jeff Jackson, firing for him. Both were working above their rank. Had they been doing the jobs for which they were trained, a qualified driver would have brought the loco into the shed with Mick firing for him, and Jeff would have cleaned the boiler and got it ready for the next round. Instead, Mick had control of 30 tons of steam engine. In the dark, Jeff got down to change the points and signalled for Mick to proceed. As Jeff ran back to jump on the footplate, he slipped and fell under the wheel. He lost a leg and Mick was dismissed for negligence.

After a bitter argument, Jack convinced the Board to reinstate Mick. He very strongly recommended they review the practice of forcing youngsters to carry out jobs beyond their years and experience. It was like that with Queensland Railway. He could only strongly recommend.

While in Rockhampton Jack, who enjoyed woodworking, made application to learn the trade of wagon builder. At the end of the first week of training he rode his bike through the front gate, steering with his right hand and holding a bulky parcel under his left arm. He dismounted at the front steps, and called Jackie and Madge to the verandah. His first task had been to construct something simple to get the feel of the saw, the plane and the hammer. Two small stools, each with a letter outlined by thumbtacks, emerged from the brown paper.

'That's mine,' said Jackie, snatching the one with the 'J'. Madge took the one with 'M' and, carrying it into the bathroom, turned on the tap that was normally beyond her reach. The next week Jack brought home a red cedar cabinet with a bevelled glass panel set into the door. All the men did it: made illegal 'foreigners' during work time.

Jack enjoyed woodwork almost as much as he enjoyed union work. In March he started work as a wagon builder on nineteen shillings a day. Life looked good.

But Jack decided it was time to move on again, and applied for a transfer to Warwick. Once again, on the move and once again, Mary was pregnant. In March 1922, Jack and Mary welcomed their third child, Hazel Mary, to the O'Leary household.

Jack joined the Warwick branch of the Australian Labor Party and attended the monthly meetings as well as the monthly meetings of the Australian Railways Union - the result of a merger of the Queensland Railways Union with the Australian Railways Union of the southern states. It was on one of his trips to Brisbane that Jack met George Rymer, the first full-time president of the new union, who encouraged Jack to become branch correspondent for its monthly broadsheet, *The Advocate*.

Jack purchased a typewriter and taught himself to type using all ten fingers. Each evening, on the kitchen table, he tapped away at his reports as well as letters to other newspapers and parliamentarians. He became known for his pro-communist leanings, although he had no desire to join the newly-formed Communist Party of Australia.

Twice weekly a local Railway Debating Society, initiated by Jack, met to debate such topics as 'The 44 Hour Week', 'Does Unionism Benefit Workers?', and the topic that affected every Australian worker who found himself competing with the low-waged Islanders - 'The White Australia Policy'.

In 1924 Jack began to scour *The Advocate* for any transfers available. Mary recognised the now familiar signs of restlessness and knew there was no stopping Jack once he had that look in his eyes. One night, as they played cribbage on a board he'd made in the Workshops, she tackled the subject.

'I think we should move to Brisbane, buy a house, and settle down,' she said. Jack looked up in surprise.

'It's obvious you want to move again. Am I right?'

'Am I that transparent, Mary?'

'Yes you are, Jack O'Leary. You were born restless. But the kids need an education, and it can't happen with us wandering all over the country.'

The union occasionally held smoke socials where the workers and their families gathered to drink, smoke and be entertained. The Warwick branch held a smoke social to farewell Jack, and every worker from the district turned up. During the evening, speaker after speaker took the floor to eulogise Jack, wishing him and his family success in Brisbane. Many made mention of his uncanny ability to represent them at hearings, and told of the bright future they foresaw for him, either as a union official or as a member of parliament. Mary had no idea her husband was such a well-liked person.

Mary was determined this would be their final move, and Jack's involvement in the union was developing at such a rate that he realised Brisbane held his future. In August of 1924 they rented a house in Logan Road near the Woolloongabba Goods Yards, where Jack began work as a wagon builder's assistant and immediately joined the Annerley Branch of the Labor Party, becoming secretary at the following party elections.

Two months later, Jack said to Mary: 'I think we should move'. He did not raise his head from the newspaper as he made the statement. Mary threw the book she was reading straight at Jack, and became angrier still when he laughed at her.

'I think we should build a house.'

It took a few seconds for the full meaning to dawn on Mary.

On a rainy day in February they settled into Belgrove, named by Mary after the street in which her family still lived in Glasgow. They were now in debt to the tune of £794. Jack set up a work-bench under the house, and within a few weeks had built a double bed from silky oak with tulip-shapes cut into the bed head. One was lop-sided, but Mary never mentioned this. They planted morning glory along the trellis against the house and roses along the path that led from the picket fence to the stairs.

≈

- PART TWO -

All men are born equal - but some descend to parliament.

E.H. Lane

Chapter 4 - The anti-Communist pledge (1925)

J ack arrived at the Woolloongabba Goods Yards to the acrid smell of burning coal exhaust from a loco's chimney. He nodded good morning to a man who, waving a red flag high with his left hand and ringing a brass bell with his right, walked into the path of trams and motor vehicles converging from all points onto the intersection known as the Woolloongabba Fiveways. The traffic paused. Steel wheels clattered over the points and, with a breathy whistle, the loco and its two carriages followed the man across the road then continued on their way to Southport.

In the goods yards, a railway carriage rolled through the open doorway and creaked to rest in the dust and gloom of the shed, awaiting repair to its weathered timbers. Jack pressed a pad of coarse-grit glass paper to the coachwood door and moved it in circles, beginning the mind-numbing task of revealing the pinkish-brown timber beneath the peeling paint. The task suited his mood today. He had not slept well worrying over this evening's meeting and so, as the day progressed, he kept one eye on the large round clock face above the doorway, willing its hands to move faster.

When the steam whistle finally released the workers from the Gabba Yards, Jack dipped into a forty-four gallon drum of water outside the shed and scrubbed his face and forearms. He grabbed his hat and gladstone bag, in his rush almost forgetting to replace his brass tag on the tag board.

He passed wooden hoppers loaded for the coal wharves at South Brisbane and followed a path, reclaimed from bluetop and cobbler's pegs by years of tramping boots, up a bank to Stanley Street just as a tram crawled to a stop. He hooked a wrist through the dangling leather loop and swayed to the tram's rhythm across Victoria Bridge to the city.

Jumping off at North Quay, he zigzagged along Adelaide Street into Edward Street. He took the steep pinch at a cracking pace, dodging motorcars, pedestrians and narrowly avoiding a delivery van and its plodding draughthorse. Without a pause to draw breath, he bounded up the front steps of Trades Hall two at a time and disappeared into its arched doorway.

Men - not just party members either - choked the internal stairwell. Jack elbowed through their wall of sweat and cigarette smoke and wedged himself between two mustachioed men blocking the doorway to meeting room forty-five. Recognising Jack, the men parted, allowing him to enter.

Jack had made it in time to vote - just.

A middle-aged man was addressing the crowd from a platform at the front of the room: 'The motion before the chair is that this branch of the ALP deplores the Central Executive's demand to expel members of the Communist Party from its ranks, and that this resolution be forwarded to all ALP branches for endorsement. Do we have a seconder?'

'Yes!'

As if pulled by a thread, all heads swivelled towards the shout from Jack at the rear of the room.

'The chair recognises Comrade O'Leary from Annerley branch. All those in favour?'

The room filled with raised arms and oaths.

'Okay men, that concludes today's business.'

Later that evening, with knees weakened by celebratory shandies, Jack jumped from a slowing tram at Chardon's Corner and wove his way home along Venner Road. He heard the scuffle of feet, caught a passing whiff of cigarette smoke, saw a pinprick of light glow red, then fade.

'You don't scare me!' He shouted into the blackness. 'Jus' fuck off!'

His words sounded more slurred than he'd wished.

~

Four weeks after the branch meeting called in support of the Communists, the ALP state organiser, Joe Collings - a man of mature years, neatly dressed in a three-piece suit, his head topped by a grey trilby - walked down a laneway and entered the public bar of the Grand Central Hotel, pausing for his eyes to adjust to its dimness after the midday glare.

He approached the bar: 'The usual, Jim'.

This place ruffled Collings' composure, but he had need of the men who frequented it. He collected his lemonade and brushed an imaginary fleck from his lapel as he perused the room, sipping from the glass.

From the far corner, shouts rose above the general hubbub where a dishevelled young man prodded the shoulder of another man, pressing him into the wall. The pinioned man threw a punch at the young man's belly then fled through the door into the lane.

Collings waited until the young man stumbled outside, doubled in pain, before placing his empty glass on the bar and following. He found the young man steadying himself with a hand on the toilet wall, vomiting into a drain that reeked of stale urine.

'Gidday Frank. Not feeling too well?'

Frank Ryan gave one final spit and attempted to stand erect. Aware of the disparity between his appearance and that of Collings, he wiped his mouth with the back of his hand and smoothed his lank hair. Before Frank could stammer a reply, Collings said: 'Got a job for you, if you're interested'.

'Yeah, I could do with a quid.'

'Tonight. Wait outside Trades Hall. The meeting should finish around eight. Take your pick, they're all bastards.'

'What if I get caught? I'll end up back in gaol.'

'It's a chance you'll have to take. But if you do get caught, we'll make sure you're given a lenient sentence.'

As Collings turned down the lane and disappeared into Elizabeth Street, Frank sank to his knees. His belly hurt as much from hunger as from the punch.

☞

That evening, as men spilled down the granite stairs of Trades Hall and gathered in pools of light on the footpath, locked in animated discussion, Frank pressed against the side wall, making himself invisible beyond the light's reach. A horse clopped past, pulling a cab, someone laughed aloud and someone else shouted.

Frank tore at the eczema rash on his neck, cursing as he drew blood. He hadn't shaved since the rash appeared a week ago, and he knew the stubble on his face added to his unkempt look. He'd scrub up before next Saturday, with his girl arriving from Sydney.

Two men peeled from the group and waved farewell.

'Goodnight Jack; goodnight Fred,' called the other men.

Frank let them pass and waited for someone to walk his way, alone. Soon, another man in a tweed jacket left the dwindling group and rounded the corner. Frank worked his fingers into a fist as the man began climbing the concrete stairs separating Trades

Hall from Wickham Park. Frank felt the gristle of the man's nose crunch beneath his knuckles, then the rough wool over his kidneys. Four quick punches and the job was done, as he had been trained to do in the days when he could still box. The man collapsed on the stairs, and Frank delivered a parting kick to his backside for good measure. He turned and ran along Turbot Street towards the river, slowing after a couple of blocks to catch his breath. A soft whistle drifted from a building. Frank approached the doorway and held out his hand.

'Where's me money?'

'How do I know you've done the job?'

Frank held his fists an inch from Collings' face. The swollen knuckles glowed pink in a light from a ground floor window.

'How the fucking hell do you think I got these?'

Collings backed away, his top lip curled in disgust. He did not like associating with this sort, but they did the jobs he couldn't do. He removed a roll of notes from his trouser pocket and unpeeled a pound note. Holding it between his thumb and forefinger as if it were contaminated, he dangled it towards Frank.

'I trust you taught him a lesson?'

'He won't be no good for nothing for a while. Left him heaving his guts up.'

Frank headed for the pub to spend his quid. Collings dissolved into the shadows.

↬

Mary looked up from her knitting to check the time on the mantle clock on the sideboard. Five to ten. She rolled the half-finished vest around the needles and stuffed it into her knitting bag. Another evening without Jack joining the family for dinner.

When Mary married Jack thirteen years ago, she knew she was taking on a union as well as a husband, but as she swatted the sticky black flies in the canvas tent of the navvy camp, she'd thought that, in time, her strong will would guide this easy-going man towards the responsibilities of domesticity. However, as she followed him from camp to workshop, from town to town - first with one child, then two, then three - he revealed a fiery determination that surpassed even hers. His father had been a union man all his working life. Some things were not negotiable. Now, as secretary of his Labor Party branch as well as his union branch, Jack spent more evenings at meetings than he did at the dinner table - especially just lately, with the state Labor Party plotting to get rid of unionists who supported the Communist Party.

Mary made ready for bed, leaving Jack's shepherd's pie in the oven, its creamy potato topping dried and cracked. If he was hungry, he could blooming well eat that!

Before turning in she stepped onto the verandah to look for signs of Jack walking from the tram. Two street lamps lit the narrow strip of bitumen that climbed the slope to the main road, passing half a dozen houses whose windows broke the blackness. She saw not one, but two hats pass below the street lamps as if playing a part in a silent movie. She raced inside and changed from her nightie back into her day clothes and emerged from the bedroom just as Jack entered the hallway with a stranger. Jack broke off mid-sentence when he saw her: 'Hello love, I didn't think you'd still be up. Sorry I'm late'.

He extended his hand towards his companion: 'This is Fred Paterson. Fred, meet my wife, Mary'.

Fred removed his hat and Mary was surprised to see thinning hair on one so young. He bent low and took her hand in his, saying in a slow drawl: 'Pleased to make your acquaintance, Mrs O'Leary. Jack's invited me to spend the night, but if it's not convenient, I can leave'.

'Not at all. If Jack offered you a bed for the night, a bed you shall have.'

Mary was charmed by the slim, unassuming man.

'Fred came down from Gladstone for the meeting,' explained Jack. 'We only met tonight, although I've heard plenty about him. The meeting room was packed, so many turned up! Come and have a cuppa with us, Mary.'

Mary joined the two men at the kitchen table and discreetly disposed of Jack's desiccated dinner.

Fred was saying: 'I'm glad you supported Moxom's resolution'.

'What resolution's that?' asked Mary.

Fred rose from the table, stood behind his chair and theatrically clasped his lapel with his right hand: 'That this branch of the ALP deplores its Executive toadying to the 'Communist bogey' propaganda by demanding the expulsion of members of the Communist Party, and that it extends a welcome to all working-class fighters whose mission it is to better the lot of their class, and that notice of this resolution be forwarded to all branches of the ALP for endorsement'.

He sat down, clearly pleased with his performance, while Jack laughed: 'Bloody hell, how did you remember all that?'

Fred winked and tapped his head: 'Photographic memory. Seriously though,' continued Fred, 'we've really got a fight ahead. I've resigned from the CPA, so they can't point the finger at me, but I bloody well refuse to sign that pledge'.

'What do you do in Gladstone, Mr Paterson?' interrupted Mary.

'I'm a pig farmer.'

This surprised Mary. He didn't look like a pig farmer.

'Why would you come all the way down here for a party meeting?'

Jack answered Mary's question: 'Fred's not *just* a pig farmer. He was a teacher, even been to university. We asked him to come down because he's a straight thinker when it comes to party issues. We value his input.'

'What about your branch Jack?' asked Fred. 'Do you have support?'

'Pretty much. None of them'll sign it.'

Mary couldn't stifle her yawns as the conversation turned to the minutia of action plans. She bade them goodnight and went to make up the spare bed in the sleep-out. She fell asleep to the drone of voices from the kitchen. When she awoke the following morning, Fred had already left to catch the train back to Gladstone. The spare bed had not been slept in and Jack was still sitting, bleary-eyed, at the kitchen table, in the centre of which lay a rose from their front garden and a note scrawled in spidery handwriting:

Mrs O'Leary, thank-you for your kind hospitality. Fred Paterson.

Mary smiled and placed the rose in a vase, but could not quell a sense of foreboding.

'I get the feeling something big's brewing,' she said as she prepared breakfast.

'Bigger than you think, Mary.'

The aroma of bubbling oats drew the three children from their bedrooms. Jackie, a freckled ten-year-old replica of his father, rocked on the rear legs of a kitchen chair, anticipating the cuff across his ear. When it came, he defiantly paused with the chair in perfect balance. Madge, two years younger than Jackie, lifted the rose to her nose to breathe its perfume. Two-year-old Hazel wriggled onto her father's lap and helped herself to his porridge.

The daily newspapers reported inner-city bashings of unionists.

૱

The dull ache of hunger in Frank Ryan's gut was of little importance as he waited at South Brisbane station for the arrival of the train carrying his sweetheart. He had stayed in a hostel overnight and now appeared freshly shaven, his hair washed and neatly parted along the centre of his scalp. He ran a finger around his high-standing collar to ease its pressure on his neck that had healed, except for a couple of persistent scabs. Resisting the urge to scratch, he bent and retrieved a butt from the platform and lit up.

The din from the waiting crowd increased as an engine eased in beside the platform, steam gushing from beneath its skirts as coachwood doors banged and red cedar windows clattered open, sprouting heads of all shapes and sizes. Travellers, weary from their thirty-hour journey, emerged seeking porters, and, from a paperboy shouting the day's headlines, swapped coins for newspapers.

Frank, who was not very tall, had trouble seeing along the platform. He dodged new arrivals and luggage trolleys, seeking Gwen. The crowd thinned before he finally caught sight of the familiar thin rounded shoulders leaning against the wall. She wore a brown cloche hat, the same colour and shape as her bobbed hair. He walked fast, broke into a trot. He had missed her since she'd been away.

He kissed her full on the mouth, ignoring the driver and fireman who whistled him on. Gwen handed him a small cardboard suitcase and tucked her arm through his bony elbow as they walked across Victoria Bridge heading for her mother's house at New Farm, three miles away. He'd try to get a meal there, although he knew he wouldn't be welcome.

Frank did not need to ask if Gwen was still his girl, despite not having seen her for six months. They shared a bond that went deeper than time and distance as each took their turn at waiting on the outside for the other to be released from gaol. This time, it had been Gwen who had been caught red-handed walking out of a Sydney store while her own discarded frock lay crumpled on the floor of the change room. She had been released on a good behaviour bond of £10 - so long as she lived with her mother for the next six months.

As they walked, Gwen lifted Frank's hand and stroked his misshapen knuckles, noticing fresh scars. He withdrew his hand and sank it into his pocket.

'Don't ask!'

Gwen walked by his side in silence.

Mrs Saunders answered the knock on the door that opened straight onto the footpath and stood, dimpled hands on ample hips, taking in the scene before her: skinny girl, scrawny boy.

'How yer doing lass?' She hugged her daughter and drew her inside. 'Suppose you'd better come in too,' she called over her shoulder to Frank.

There were only two rooms to the house. Gwen's mother parted the cotton curtain hanging across the doorway to the bedroom and tossed the suitcase between two single beds.

She returned to the living room-cum-kitchen.

'Go wash up for dinner.'

Frank and Gwen went to the washhouse beyond the back stairs. They returned to slabs of bread and a pot of dripping placed on a table that nearly filled the tiny living room.

'Eat this, then I want to see the back of you.'

Frank knew it was useless to argue. Mrs Saunders knew it was useless to forbid her daughter to keep company with Frank Ryan.

They ate in silence.

❧

The day was particularly warm for May, but the warmth did not penetrate the thick sandstone walls of Parliament House. Cigar smoke and furniture polish hung heavy in the stuffy room. A sharp rap sounded on the solid wooden door but Bill McCormack, standing by a closed window, continued watching the lunchtime crowd toss crusts to the ducks in the lily ponds of the Botanical Gardens across the road.

He removed his round, wire-framed spectacles, breathed on each lens in turn and polished them with his handkerchief. Only after he replaced his glasses did he call: 'Yes?'.

The door flung open, admitting a breeze and Joe Collings. In the distance, a bell sounded throughout the building, summoning a division of the House.

The tip of a cigar, balanced on the rim of a glass ashtray, glowed with the breeze, gave up one final wisp of smoke, and faded. McCormack turned from the window - much smaller than the one through which he would look when he became Premier of Queensland - to face his visitor.

Each man eyed the other through deep-set eyes topped by bushy eyebrows; but while Joe Collings, with his aristocratic curve of nose and trim grey beard, was almost good-looking, Bill McCormack's thinning hair and bulky build bespoke the working class origins which had brought him within grasp of the state premiership.

'What's your plan, Joe? I assume you have one.'

'I'm playing with some ideas Mac, and I shall brief you on those at a later date; they are long term and require careful planning. However, I thought our immediate concern should be to ensure every party member signs the anti-Communist pledge.'

On the far side of the desk sat another man whose full lips would have been considered sensuous had they not curved into a supercilious sneer sometime in his youth, twenty years before. Ted Theodore had come a long way since taking his place as a scruffy young man in the Queensland Parliament in 1909. Knowing he was a poor speaker, he had devoted eighteen months to speech lessons. He now dressed with care, easing his solid frame into a neat suit, and always wore a bowler hat over a head of black hair, to which graying temples added a distinguished touch.

He retrieved the cigar from the ashtray and offered a flame to its end, sending a stream of thick smoke into the air.

Joe Collings stood between the two, checking that the knot of his silk tie sat equidistant between the curves of his collar, awaiting the invitation to be seated that never came.

'What's the plan then, Joe?' Theodore didn't look at Collings; he rarely looked directly at anyone.

'I have studied all the facts, and in my considered opinion, we need to target the ARU,' replied Collings.

McCormack's frown deepened at the mention of the militant railways union and anger distorted his thin mouth. He smoothed his receding hair from a low side parting. By rights, he should have been Premier by now; that was the plan when Ted had resigned, until that bloody union threw a spanner in the works. He waited for the state organiser to continue.

'A considerable number of the rank-and-file are communist sympathisers and, I suspect, will not sign the pledge. The best plan is to rid the party of such unsavoury elements,' replied Collings.

Theodore, who had long ago grown tired of Collings' verbosity, cut him short: 'We'll wait and see what results we get when the returns are lodged. If they don't sign we'll expel them!'

Theodore waved his hand. Collings considered himself dismissed.

Ted Theodore nipped the end from his cigar and tucked it into the pocket of his waistcoat, donned his bowler hat, collected his cane, and took his leave. He crossed the road and entered the double iron gates to the Botanical Gardens where he could wander and think undisturbed. It was a walk he took often.

Children climbed, elfin-like, through the other-worldliness of the roots that hung in curtains from the banyan tree. He chose the path that led away from their intrusive laughter.

Theodore had big plans for his Party. Much as a man emerges from boyhood, it had outgrown the socialist shackles of its formative years and was forging new liaisons that would do neither the party nor himself any harm: he and Mac had convinced the government to purchase Lady Jane and Girofla mines at Mungana - and no one suspected they had an interest in the business.

However, in tandem with the Party's growth had come unrest from the voters who believed the communist bogey stories regularly appearing in *The Brisbane Courier*. If the Party was to win the state election next year it had to slough off unions like the Australian Railways Union that kept dragging it back to its roots.

Having outgrown state politics, Theodore was bound for Canberra. John Wren, the son of a poor Irish immigrant who had risen to become one of Australia's most influential businessmen with the ability to manipulate the political scene, had assured Theodore it was as good as done. However, politically, Theodore was now a loose wheel, although he looked forward with high expectation to the federal election in November. He had resigned his premiership in February - having won pre-selection for the Federal seat of Herbert the previous July; but Mac, who was supposed to step into his shoes, had missed out on the leadership by one vote to Gillies. He would need to bring his considerable influence to bear to fix that, and soon.

The trill of a bell brought Theodore back to the present and two young people swept past either side on bicycles, bracketing his thoughts. He stepped onto the verandah of the kiosk atop a rise near the Domain and sat at a table beneath the gabled roof. He ordered a pot of tea and retrieved the cigar from his waistcoat pocket. A matronly woman in a crisp white apron set a china teapot on the table and laid a silver tea strainer across the top of a cup.

'Will that be all Mr Theodore?'

The charm that made him a successful politician in the past softened his features.

'Thank you Alice. That's all for now.'

She left him alone to watch the game of croquet in progress on the lawn in front of the kiosk. His mind slowed as a young man swung a mallet back between his feet and sent the wooden ball hopping across the grass.

~

Chapter 5 - To sign, or not (1925-1926)

Three months had passed since the Central Executive of the Labor Party had insisted each member sign the anti-Communist pledge or be expelled. To date, no one had been expelled, and so the union concentrated on other issues that threatened their members.

Three years before, in 1922, the Queensland government had gone on a cost-cutting spree: retrenching railway workers, then reducing the weekly wage of the rest by five shillings. What rankled most was that it had been a Labor Premier, Ted Theodore, who instigated the move. Relations had remained strained between the Labor Party and the Australian Railways Union in the three years since 1922. Cost cutting continued, and maintenance gangs continually claimed the tracks were unsafe. Then the Rockhampton mail train left the rails, spectacularly capsizing across the Traveston Bridge. Ten passengers were killed and twenty-eight injured.

Boilermakers at the Ipswich Workshops, incensed by the decision of the Arbitration Court to ignore their claim to a five-shilling rise in their weekly pay, had recently met outside the gates. During the meeting, the Commissioner for Railways ordered the gates locked. The next day, all workers at the Workshops assembled for a stop-work meeting in support of the boilermakers. They, too, were locked out. The various railway unions in Queensland decided enough was enough, and combined to call a halt to what they saw as the government's callous disregard for their well-being and safety. The strike committee, with support from every railway unionist in Queensland, met at Trades Hall to work on the fine details.

ఞ

Jack swept a paintbrush back and forth across the smooth coachwood timber depositing its red-brown load in four-inch strips. Tiny bubbles of paint flicked from its bristles to land, camouflaged, amongst the freckles on his face and arms, but he barely noticed; his mind was elsewhere.

The whistle sounded for smoko, and Jack rinsed his brush in a can of mud-coloured turps and wiped the flecks from his arms with a rag. Outside the carriage shed he joined two work mates, Ted Rickard and Cec Armitage sitting on a pile of discarded railway sleepers, watching a loco rotate high on a turntable at the Main Street end of the yards. It shunted back along the line running parallel with Vulture Street and came to rest below a coal stage where a railwayman steered a half-ton skip from a bin and tipped it towards the loco's tender. A flap opened at the end of the skip and the load of coal clattered out amidst a cloud of black dust.

Tom turned to Jack: 'So, are we going out tonight?'

'Word is, at midnight,' replied Jack who, recently elected to the committee of the South-eastern District of the union, was to sit on the strike committee. Cec grinned: 'Serves 'em bloody right! Think they can fuck around with our wages!'

Jack passed the word to other men at lunchtime while they chewed over sandwiches and the conundrum of the Ipswich lockout. The word spread from worker to worker until the whole of the Gabba Yards, except the bosses, knew not to turn up from midnight.

Jack did not sleep when he arrived home late from another strike committee meeting. As the clock chimed midnight and every train in Queensland ground to a halt, he put his arm around Mary and said: 'It's showdown time, love'.

~

Jack approached Trades Hall the next morning to find Edward Street choked with a couple of thousand railwaymen, and at 9.30 they headed off along Albert Street towards the Brisbane Stadium. Waving above the procession, at intervals, placards promised *Solidarity For Ever*; periodically someone shouted: 'Are we downhearted?' and the response came loud and strong: 'No!' By the time they entered the Stadium, their numbers had swollen to 5,000 with onlookers drawn into the stream of determined protesters. Filing into the Stadium, the strikers paid no heed to the fact that the building was owned by John Wren: mate of Ted Theodore; sporting tycoon; dubious Labor patron who employed his considerable influence in the labour movement against the Left - but who allowed his premises to be used for gatherings and protests.

A shaft of sunlight shone through the gap below the mansard roof and settled onto the boxing ring from which the ropes had been removed, leaving a wooden platform with posts rising from each corner. Jack stepped onto the platform and took a seat beside the union's state president, George Rymer, its secretary, Tim Moroney, and Fred Paterson who, upon hearing of the strike, had left his pigs and caught the next train to Brisbane.

As Jack, who had been nominated to open the meeting, rose and moved to the front of the platform, the buzz of conversation hushed to hear him speak. Journalists from *The Daily Standard* and *The Brisbane Courier*, seated in the front row, noted every word. Each would put his own bias to his report.

Comrades, it is wonderful to see such strong support. I promise, you won't be disappointed. I emphasise that we're all workers who insist upon the right to live. The strike committee has decided to concentrate on just two points - the five per cent pay rise and the right to hold stop-work meetings. I know there're other issues that some of you would like addressed. When we go back to work we can begin the fight for these.

Since 1922 the right to live decently has been refused to us. Judges have been appointed, at £10 a week, to tell us, the workers, to live on £4.

I implore you to smash the capitalistic press that's falsely reporting our struggle and trying to create a schism in our ranks. Think positively of the future, is my advice. Our wives and children will be better off.

Jack resumed his seat to deafening cheers. The corners of his mouth turned into a smile.

Questions were asked...

'What about the livestock held up in railway carriages?'

... and answers given:

'There's an army of volunteers ready to feed and water them daily, and will continue to do so as long as the strike continues.'

'How'll we feed ourselves?'

'A strike fund is being initiated, and assistance is available for anyone who needs it.'

'What about transporting emergency provisions?'

'If necessary, use horses instead of locos to pull the loads. That's how they're drawing the coal to the wharf at Gladstone.'

The men voted overwhelmingly to continue the strike until they achieved their aims. Everyone rose and broke into the singing of 'The Red Flag'.

The next day, Mary surprised Jack by announcing: 'I'd like to come this morning'.

'Why?'

'Wouldn't you like moral support?'

'Well yes, it just seems out of character.'

'I know that, but when I do see you, the strike's all you can talk about, so I may as well be there to see for myself.'

'You'll have to make your own way there. I've got to go to Trades Hall first.'

'That's all right. I'll catch a tram when Jackie and Madge have left for school.'

Jack gulped down his breakfast, kissed Mary goodbye, and dashed off.

Mary, standing proud within her five feet and one-and-a-half inches, studied her reflection in the wardrobe mirror, not for effect - she knew the new dress suited her - rather to check for signs of puckered seams or uneven hemline, the tell-tale signs that the garment was home-made. Satisfied, she set off for town with Hazel. Without the trains running, the tram to town was packed. Mary glanced around her, trying to guess which passengers were on their way to the strike meeting.

As they approached Stanley Street in South Brisbane, a large, rough-looking man got in and sat opposite her. He wore a union badge on his collarless flannel shirt. Surreptitiously, Mary tried to see which union, but her eyesight was too poor. He caught her looking and gave a wide grin, exposing broken teeth and, she was sure, bad breath. Mary looked away, blushing under his smile. Probably a wharfie, she thought to herself.

The tram rattled on its way. More passengers came on board. Mary sat Hazel on her knee to make room. Passengers, with outstretched hands hanging from the leather loops, fell against each other as the tram jerked its way between the arches of Victoria Bridge.

One three-year-old voice rose above the conversations and, legs swinging in time with the familiar tune, Hazel held centre stage:

'Arise, ye workers from your slumbers ...'

The wharfie gave an even wider grin, and winked knowingly. Everyone laughed and some joined in the song. Mary was embarrassed, but amused.

The tram stopped in Queen Street, and all but a few passengers got off and headed along Albert Street towards the Stadium. Again, there was a record crowd.

The strike lasted eight days and altered life over the whole of Brisbane. At every strike meeting, from Brisbane to Rockhampton, Fred Paterson addressed the strikers.

Jack spoke at mass meetings at Wickham Park, at Roma Street, at Trades Hall and at the Stadium. Day after day the streets of Brisbane filled with men marching, red flag up front, from their workplaces to the meetings. They all knew that a win by the railwaymen would strengthen their own claims to better living and working conditions.

The Brisbane press published photos of the Gabba men en route to Roma Street, as well as the mass meetings. The Labor paper, *The Daily Standard*, which had reprinted Jack's opening speech at the Stadium rally, reported on the struggle day by day.

Each morning Jack bought the papers on his way to Trades Hall. Each evening he sat at the kitchen table while Mary prepared dinner, and read the articles aloud, gloating or ranting, depending on the bias of the paper: *The Brisbane Courier* against the workers, *The Daily Standard* for the workers.

On 4 September Premier Gillies capitulated and restored the five shillings previously lost by the 1922 arbitration decision. He also declared that workers had the right to hold stop work meetings.

Jack returned to the daily grind of work at the Gabba Yards, but looked forward to the day when he could join the union's executive full time and do more than simply represent fellow workers at the Arbitration Court and on strike committees.

᠗

Jack arrived early at the hall to prepare for the Annerley Branch meeting on the evening of 12 October. There was only one motion on the agenda and it was in his interests to see it succeed. He lined the wooden chairs in rows facing the table around which the executive would sit, and welcomed each member as he arrived. When the room was full, Jack opened the meeting and read his motion: 'I move that this meeting of the Annerley branch of the ALP emphatically protests against the low-down tactics in compelling candidates to sign the pledge when they have already signed the constitution'.

He then addressed the meeting: 'In opening the floor to discussion on this motion, I would like to say that I intend to seek pre-selection for the seat of Logan for the next election. We, as a branch, have already voted to take a stand and ignore the QCE's directive to sign the anti-Communist pledge at the risk of being expelled. A new directive now demands that anyone standing for pre-selection *must* sign the pledge, or be refused candidature. Does anyone wish to speak against the motion?'

Another member seconded the motion, and it was carried unanimously. Jack visibly relaxed.

Just as he was ready to call the meeting to a close, a man rose from the back of the room.

'I've been thinking, Mr Secretary: wouldn't it be better if you sign the new pledge, but do it under protest until it goes to Convention next year? That way, you can still stand for pre-selection.'

'Are you making it a motion?' asked Jack.

'Yes.'

'Do we have a seconder?'

That motion, too, was passed, clearing the way for Jack to put his name forward for pre-selection later that month. The following week, Gillies faced a no-confidence motion and McCormack became Premier of Queensland, firming Jack's decision to stand. When he made the announcement to Mary, she paused mid-row and placed the knitting needles on her lap.

'I thought you wanted to be on the union executive!'

'Yes, I do. And I will one day, but that's taking too long. If I'm in parliament, I can keep a closer eye on McCormack and his dirty tricks.'

'And what about your secret?'

They never spoke directly of Jack's court-martial, but they both knew it was a tool that could be used by those who didn't want him to succeed politically.

'That was seven years ago, I doubt anyone knows about it, but it's a chance I'll take.'

Mary resumed knitting and the needles clacked faster than usual.

'Well, if that's what you want, I can't stop you.'

'No, but I'd like to know I had your blessing.'

'Jack O'Leary, you don't need my blessing. Just get on with it.'

~

As the deadline for signatures on the anti-Communist pledge drew near, Labor Party state organiser, Joe Collings, barricaded himself in the party's executive office in Elizabeth Street and counted returns lodged from the Queensland branches. Of a total of three hundred branches, only eighty-two had agreed to sign willingly. Three branches had refused to sign. One was the Annerley Branch. Jack O'Leary, whose nomination for pre-selection had recently arrived at party headquarters, was secretary of the Annerley branch and it had not escaped Joe Collings' notice that he was also an emerging figure within the Australian Railways Union.

Collings picked up the phone and dialled the number of the union office. A woman with well-rounded vowels answered, and he asked to speak to the secretary of the South-eastern District.

The single ring of the phone startled John Hayes, seated at his desk contemplatively chewing on the stub of a pencil. He lifted the earpiece.

'Collings here. Drop in to the party office next time you're passing, John, there's something I want to discuss with you.'

'Okay Joe. Will tomorrow do?'

'Tomorrow would be good.'

Hayes replaced the earpiece, puzzled by the phone call.

He enjoyed his newly-elected position of secretary for the South-eastern District. It had meant moving from Townsville, but he never liked the cloying heat of that place anyway. All his life he had lived in the northern part of the state: Chillagoe, Townsville, back to Chillagoe to relieve long-time organiser Bill Morrow for a spell - and in the meantime failing to be pre-selected for the state seat - then back to Townsville. He wanted to make something of himself, and Brisbane was the place to do it. He moved into a nice home in Albion, with a verandah along two sides. And Joe Collings could be of use, he was sure, as he always was.

Collings replaced the receiver on its cradle. He was sure he would be able to discourage O'Leary, but it didn't hurt to take out extra insurance. It was part of his plan.

He re-counted the returns, just in case he'd made a mistake, but he had not.

He then penned a letter to the Central Executive asking for the expulsion of the pro-Communist Jack O'Leary who would waste no time in letting Russians and IWW members into the Labor Party, given half a chance.

❧

Jack returned home late on Saturday night, not entirely sober. One look at his face, and Mary knew he'd lost the plebiscite.

'Brown won,' he said, even before she could ask. Mary walked over to give him a consoling hug, but the smell of alcohol repelled her. She turned to stoke the fire. When she straightened, Jack had left the room. She looked in the bathroom, the bedroom, but couldn't find him. He'd gone out again. Angry, she went to bed.

When she arose the next morning, he was sitting on the back steps, deep in thought.

'Do you want porridge?'

He looked up at her but his eyes had lost their fire.

'Please sit with me, Mary. I need to talk.'

She sat on the step above him.

'I think the bastards are winning, Mary. After they announced the results of the pre-selection, Collings came over to me and said, "Outside, O'Leary!" I followed him onto the footpath and he said, "Right O'Leary, your days are numbered. I've got the dirt on you, and if you so much as try to stand for pre-selection again, it'll all come out".' Jack paused. 'Problem is Mary, I don't know if he was referring to the court-martial or not. He may have just been referring to the pledge.'

'Every time you're reminded of the war, you get drunk. Can't you forget about it?'

'Yeah, well, sometimes it's what a bloke needs to help him forget.'

ॐ

Ted Theodore didn't campaign very aggressively for the federal elections that month. He was, John Wren assured him, needed in Canberra. It would be a pushover. Theodore always listened to this man of awe-inspiring influence; and so Theodore concentrated his energy on sorting out the worsening situation at state level, spending minimal time on the campaign trail.

Neither he nor Wren had bargained on the power of the union. Theodore lost the seat of Herbert by 268 votes - about the same number of railway workers in the electorate - and there was a large number of informal votes. Theodore knew why they'd done it: they were getting even with him for knocking the five bob off their wages back in '22.

ॐ

Approaching 35, John Hayes still had the physique of a twenty-year-old, and he knew it. All his life he had been a sportsman and kept in shape, and he wore his long sleeves rolled up to his biceps, of which he was proud. In every way, he was the antithesis of the man who sat on the other side of the desk. Gentlemanly and scholarly, Joe Collings walked with a slight stoop which he'd carried since his sixtieth birthday. Working class to his bootlaces, John Hayes carried his 6-foot frame tall, and his clipped dark curly hair had never seen a hat.

Collings offered his silver cigarette case to the younger man: 'How are you settling into the new job, John?'

John helped himself to a cigarette and was surprised when Collings leant across the desk to light it for him.

'Can't complain. You know. They've given me a good office in Trades Hall.'

'Do they leave you alone to make decisions?'

'Hell no! I do what I'm told.'

'That's a pity. A man of your talents should be given free rein. If you were secretary in the Australian Workers Union, you'd be given space to shine.'

John drew on his cigarette, buying time. The words coming from Collings sounded awfully like a bribe. Collings continued: 'The ARU is too narrow; they want all the other railway unions to combine to form one big Union. I'm sure you've heard all the propaganda.'

'Well, yes, but it makes sense. Gives the unions more clout.'

It was exactly this clout that Collings and his mate Mac feared. He could see he needed to tread delicately here.

'I think you'll find that the AWU has more 'clout', as you put it, seeing they are much better represented in the Labor Party, and that's where policy is made. The country will be much better off with the craft unions joining up with the AWU. Fewer strikes, less industrial unrest.'

'Are you offering me a job?'

'Not directly. But if you could keep your ear to the ground and let me know of any unrest in your union, we would see you right.'

'By "we", you mean you and McCormack?'

'Mac is keen to advance the Railways Division of the AWU.'

John extinguished his cigarette in the glass ashtray. Joe Collings rose to open the door.

'Think it over, John.'

John left the secretary's office with his ear to the ground - as instructed.

෨

Since moving to Brisbane, Jack had struck up a close friendship with his union's president, George Rymer, the diminutive, softly-spoken Englishman who sported a bushy black moustache and with whom Jack had much in common. They had both sailed to Australia from the other side of the world as young men, bringing their passion for union activity with them: Jack from the coalmines of south Wales, George from the railways of England.

While the same degree of friendship did not exist between Jack and the union's state secretary, Tim Moroney, each held the other in respect, and the three men often met to discuss union strategies, to the annoyance of John Hayes who was excluded. Tim and George became regular visitors to Jack and Mary's home, and made no secret of the fact they would like Jack to join the executive, should an opportunity arise.

At the November meeting of the Central Executive of the Labor Party, the union was represented by Jack, along with George, Tim and John Hayes. Immediately the meeting opened, McCormack - targeting the union officials - moved a motion that anyone present who had not signed the anti-Communist pledge be thrown out. Tim Moroney objected: he said he wasn't about to give the Central Executive unlimited power to gerrymander, or interfere with the rules. But the meeting jeered him and told him to sit down.

Tim and George refused outright to sign, but John Hayes walked up to the registration desk and signed the pledge. Jack,

Tim and George left Hayes at the meeting and, amid further jeers, walked from the room.

But the union was skating on thin ice and, if it was to be involved in Labor Party policy development at the Labor-in-Politics Convention in February, needed to sort out its position regarding the signing of the anti-Communist pledge.

The State Council of the union met for four days in January, and Jack organised time-off to attend each session as an observer. On the final morning, Jack woke early after a restless night.

'Can't you sleep?' Mary asked.

The weather was unbearably hot. They lay on top of the sheets, their night clothes sticking to their legs; the curtain hung limply over the bedroom window, not a breath of air to stir it. The sun had only been up half an hour, but already its heat penetrated their bedroom.

Jack sat on the edge of the bed, coughing. Mary watched his thin back straining, the ribs working beneath his skin. He was doing that a lot lately. If this was a cold, it was taking its time passing.

'No, I can't sleep. My mind's racing. I'll go and get my papers in order for today.'

'Do you think they would mind if I came along too?'

Jack turned to her, surprised.

'Do you really want to come?'

'Whether we want it to or not, this whole business is affecting our lives. This appears to be important, and for once I'd like to be there to hear for myself.'

'Well, if it's what you want, of course you can come. Mind you, you won't be able to say anything, just observe.'

'I wouldn't know what to say anyway. No, I'll be happy just to sit and watch.'

Jack leant over and kissed her.

'Thanks for the support. Now you try to get a little more sleep.'

They caught the tram to the city. Mary had not been to the new Trades Hall, although she'd seen its imposing edifice at the top of Edward Street. Many unions had their offices in the building and many important decisions were made there. With an over-active imagination, Mary thought she could smell the power within its walls as they entered through the arched front doorway.

Jack pressed the button to open the heavy steel door to the lift. They stepped in, and it closed behind them with an echoing clang. As the cage jerked up through the centre of the building, Jack said: 'Some bloke got jammed in these doors, you know. He was leaving when his briefcase caught and they closed on him. He was quite badly injured.'

'Your timing isn't very good. I wish you hadn't told me that while we're in the lift.'

'Oh, it's all right, so long as you're quick. Personally, I preferred the manual lift. Don't know why they had to install a new-fangled automatic one.'

At the third floor, the lift shuddered to a halt, the doors slid open, and Mary leapt out quickly. They went through the door to the meeting room already half filled with hats, mostly men's, but Mary spied a few ladies' hats scattered throughout the crowd. Cigarette smoke danced in the sunlight pouring in from the high windows opposite. On a raised platform at the far end of the room was a long table, encircled by sixteen chairs. As Jack and Mary entered, George waved from the front and came over to speak to them.

'Hello Mary. Hello Jack. Collings is going to be here today. We want him to answer a few questions. Be careful, Jack. Leave it to us, even if your name comes up.'

'Is it likely to?'

'Probably. We want to show him up for what he really is.'

George returned to the table and occupied the seat in the middle. The full council of the union took its place at the table, and George tapped his glass with a pencil to bring the meeting to order.

'Welcome to day four of State Council for the Australian Railways Union.'

First item on the agenda was the election of delegates for Convention, and there was no question that Tim as secretary and George as president should represent the union. But wording of the motion regarding signing the anti-Communist pledge proved ambiguous. Comrade Hartley moved 'That this Council endorses the action of Comrades Rymer and Moroney in refusing to sign the anti-Communist pledge as members of the Central Executive'.

This motion was seconded and carried. Then, following heated discussion, Comrade McLary moved an amendment 'That the pledge be attached to the credentials of all ARU delegates and that we recommend to all ARU members present at Convention that they sign under protest subject to ratification or otherwise'.

But before a vote could be taken, another comrade got to his feet: 'I move that in order to have ARU representation at Convention, we suggest to our delegates that in the event of their finding difficulty in remaining at the Convention, they be requested to sign the pledge.'

Tim interjected angrily: 'The question to be decided is whether we should or shouldn't sign the pledge. This Council has already said we were right in not signing the pledge as union representatives to the ALP Central Executive. Now you're saying we're to sign it! If we were right in not bowing to the Central Executive in the first instance, there's no reason why we should bow to them at the Convention!'

He resumed his seat and folded his arms over his ample stomach. McLary answered him saying: 'The rank and file of the union has to be considered. The signing of the pledge now does not indicate any loss of dignity.'

A further amendment was foreshadowed: 'That we deplore the decision of the Labor Party's Central Executive for delegates to sign the anti-Communist pledge; but rather than allowing this reactionary body to "put one over" our delegates, we instruct our delegates to sign the pledge under protest'.

George finally called some order to the meeting and asked for a division on the amendment moved by Comrade McLary, resulting in a 7:5 vote in favour.

The amendment was carried and became the motion. And yet more amendments came.

By the time a vote was called for there was utter confusion in the room, except for the sixteen men seated around the committee table who knew exactly what they were voting for. The motion was carried. Tim and George felt it imprudent to cast a vote.

Another asked Hayes to offer an explanation as to why he had signed the pledge, but Hayes refused to speak. He had his ear to the ground, and the ground was beginning to rumble. Besides, he had written his reasons in last month's *Advocate*: he didn't want to disenfranchise 11,000 railway workers. That should keep them happy.

The break for morning tea came as a relief. As Mary and Jack resumed their seats for the next session a man of medium height, with a head of silver hair and an arrogant air, entered the room and, without acknowledging a soul, walked to the front and took a seat.

Mary looked at Jack who confirmed her suspicions with a silently mouthed 'Joe Collings'. She responded with an equally silent 'Oh!'.

George tapped his glass again.

'I notice Mr Joe Collings, state organiser of the ALP, is in attendance and I would like to welcome him to the meeting.'

The silver head tilted slightly in acknowledgment. George continued: 'Comrade Foley, I believe you wish to address the meeting at this point'. George sat down and Ted Foley, thin and round-shouldered, took the floor.

'Thank you, Mr President. Mr Collings is present as a result of correspondence between this union and the Labor Party. We have repeatedly asked the Central Executive to instruct the state organiser to promote the cause of industrial unionism when addressing meetings of party branches or affiliated unions. Mr Collings butted into the matter and evidently wants to appear to be the Big Man. He responded in language totally uncalled for, and I take strong exception to this. I have invited him to address this meeting to explain his position.'

Mary found all this a bit boring, but she enjoyed the way the back of Joe Collings' neck turned a bright shade of red. Ted Foley eased into his speech and gained momentum.

'Mr Collings has always carried out a policy of bluff and has always got away with it, but if he thinks that this union can be bounced like the party branches, he has made a huge mistake.'

Everyone in the room cheered, some whistled. Joe Collings sat rigidly in his seat, his hands working tensely.

'Mr Collings says he never fails to push Labor's objective, but it's my opinion that he spends hours quoting statistics relating to cost of living and wages. If he thinks that all this flap-doodle is propagating Labor's objective, we cannot agree with him.'

'Hear, hear!'

Encouraged, Foley powered on.

'I have never heard Mr Collings say one word in favour of industrial unionism since becoming organiser of the Labor Party; but the Collings of today is not the Collings of yesterday. This is a man workers once looked up to, a man who held the workers together during the 1912 Strike. Now he propagates the views of the craft union officials of the party executive instead of those of the rank and file. The executive's rejection of militant unionists shows how they think. I would like to quote the case of Comrade Jack O'Leary who has been a keen industrial and political fighter.'

Mary sat up, looked at Jack who was blushing under his freckles, and focused her attention.

'It was Mr Collings who objected to him as a candidate for pre-selection. Any man who could object to Comrade O'Leary is not doing the right thing by Labor. Comrade O'Leary is the victim of the heresy hunt against unionists who speak the truth regarding Labor's policy. It indicates the depths to which the Central Executive will descend in order to see that the 'right' man - from their point of view - wins the plebiscite.'

People clapped and turned around to Jack, smiling their support.

'The Labor Party Executive cannot be trusted to instruct Mr Collings properly.'

Ted Foley resumed his seat, and the room erupted enthusiastically. George held his hands high, palms outwards, waiting for the crowd to settle.

'Mr Collings, do you wish to address the meeting?'

Collings remained in his seat for a few moments wondering what he could possibly say to this room full of railwaymen who despised him. Slowly he rose, moved to the platform, and addressed the chair.

'Mr President, I do not propose to follow Comrade Foley. Further, I wish to enter a protest against the procedure adopted here today. I understood I was to address this meeting on behalf of the Australian Labor Party. Obviously, I have been brought here under false pretences.'

Collings turned to address the rest of the room. His voice rose in pitch.

'Mr Foley has charged me with all the crimes in Labor's calendar. I am not here on trial. The suggestion that I want to pose as the strong-man is wrong.'

Mary watched Jack shifting in his seat. Obviously he thought this man was a strong-man.

'I've come to the meeting to protest against an injustice and when that's done, I'll leave. Mr Foley has not told the truth about the O'Leary case. I have not done what is alleged. As organiser, I had to know that O'Leary had succeeded in getting the Annerley branch to carry a resolution against the pledge. The Executive asked that if anything was known against any candidate for a plebiscite, it be raised before any of the nominations were dealt with.'

For a horrible moment, Mary thought this man was about to expose Jack's court-martial. She glanced to her side, and Jack took her hand and held it tightly.

'I lodged my objection to Comrade O'Leary at the proper time. I informed them that he had succeeded in getting a branch of the Labor Party to rebel against the Executive by not signing the pledge.'

Jack and Mary breathed a collective sigh. Jack replaced her hand on her knees. Collings left the stage to catcalls and jeers, and as he drew level with their seats, fixed his eyes on Jack. His face distorted by personal animosity, he left the room.

As they broke for lunch, Jack said, 'There's no need for you to stay if you don't want to. The rest will be something of an anti-climax after that.'

'I think I will go home, if that's all right. I'm happy with what I've heard.'

༄

The debate on whether to sign the pledge or not continued for weeks within the union: to do so would be to compromise their principles; to refuse to do so would disenfranchise 11,000 Queensland railway workers from representation at the forthcoming Labor-in-Politics Convention.

As the date for Convention drew near, Jack's union did all it could to prepare for the fracas that would doubtless accompany their delegates' attendance. They paid the fees in advance and drew up a modified pledge to attach, as required, to their credentials.

Boldly typed across the pledge were the words:

> The QCE has no authority under the Rules of the ALP (State of Queensland) to demand this pledge. It is therefore signed under the protest of and on instructions of the State Council of the ARU.

Tim had just two weeks before leaving for the Labor Party Convention to be held at Southport: two weeks to clean up the correspondence that had accumulated during the week he sat on Council; attend to the correspondence arising out of Council; dictate to Miss Petfield 34 pages of scribbled notes from the rough minute book - jobs that normally took three to four weeks to complete.

The copies of the minutes were not ready until the Friday Tim was to leave for Southport. With an uneasy feeling that he had not checked them, as was his habit, he left Miss Petfield to complete the District Committees' copies and post them to all members.

On Monday morning John Hayes opened the thick envelope on his desk and read the Council minutes. When he reached page 12, he paused, puzzled. Something was not right.

That same morning, Tim and George arrived at the Southport Convention prepared for battle. They approached the registration desk and handed over their credentials beneath which were their specially prepared pledges, duly signed, and waited for the official to react. Which he did.

'Wait here.'

He disappeared through a door behind the desk into the hall and headed straight for McCormack. Tim and George watched as the big man's face grew red.

The official returned to his desk: 'These credentials have been ruled out of order. You are not permitted to attend Convention'.

He handed the papers back to the two union delegates and turned his attention to the next man in the queue.

There was no way in. Tim and George returned to Brisbane.

৵

During convention, the combined forces of McCormack's men and the Australian Workers Union carried votes of sixty-four to fourteen that stifled any opposition to the status quo. It was in all the newspapers.

Tim returned to his office early on Tuesday morning, before anyone else arrived. He hung up his coat and hat and placed his briefcase beside his desk, in the middle of which lay the 34 neatly typed pages of the minutes of State Council. He commenced reading them, just as he had dictated them last Thursday. When he reached page 12, he froze.

'Miss Petfield!'

No one answered. He was alone in the office. He re-read the final motion:

The motion then before the chair, reading as follows:-

That the pledge be attached to the credentials of all A.R.U. delegates.

He rubbed his hand across his eyes, but no matter how hard he blinked, the missing words - and that they sign under protest - would not materialise.

৵

When John Hayes arrived at his office a little after nine, he noticed Tim bending over the rough minutes book with Miss Petfield, pointing to something written in the margin. She flicked through her shorthand notebook and read out loud what had been dictated.

'I'm sorry Mr Moroney, but it's definitely not there.'

'It must be, woman!'

She turned the pad towards him.

'I can't read that gobbledegook! Come into my office and I'll dictate it again.'

The next day, all the district secretaries were issued with a new page 12, containing the motion in full, and ordered to return the incorrect version to the head office.

Hayes walked to Joe Collings' office and entered without knocking.

'You said keep my ear to the ground, well, take a look at this!'

He threw the two page twelves onto Collings' desk.

'Can we use it?' asked the party organiser.

'Bloody oath we can!'

❧

Chapter 6 - McCormack must go! (1926)

George didn't find his job as president of the Australian Railways Union very demanding: most of the day-to-day union work fell to secretary Tim. He did, however, find his position as editor of *The Advocate* most rewarding.

Many in Queensland regarded the union's monthly paper as the only reliable source of news, especially since *The Daily Standard*, the long-time paper of the Labor Party, grew more biased towards the opinions of the Party and its favoured union, the Australian Workers Union.

George curried favour with no one, so when rumours involving his *bête noire*, Bill McCormack, percolated down from the far northern town of Chillagoe, he pricked up his ears.

Without any hard evidence to back his claims, he penned an article about shady dealings at Mungana Mines, suggesting that McCormack had influenced the government to purchase the derelict mines of Lady Jane and Girofla for £40,000. He further implied that the Premier carried a personal interest in the mines.

For days George sat behind the desk in his office within Trades Hall, stroking his generous black moustache, weighing up the impact of various headlines.

He finally decided on 'McCormack Must Go!' and sat back and waited for the shit to hit the fan.

જી

The seductive aroma of ministerial leather filled the office. Reflections of dark clouds threatening to dump their load on the city streets of Brisbane floated across a wall of glass encasing rows of leather-bound volumes.

Premier McCormack stood by his large window, but he did not see the lunchtime crowd dashing for cover from the Gardens in George Street two floors below. He was barely aware of the other three men in the room.

Collings finished reading aloud the front page of *The Advocate* and handed it back to Hayes who waited with dark coat, dark hair and even darker demeanour. When he had seen what his boss had written about Mac, he'd folded the paper and headed straight for the Premier's office. As soon as McCormack glimpsed the headlines, he had summoned Collings and Theodore.

Now Hayes took the paper from Collings and attempted to reduce its impact by folding and stuffing it into his coat pocket, unaware that the words 'McCormack Must Go!' still protruded from his pocket.

Theodore, the only one in the room to remain seated, shifted uncomfortably in his chair. He felt genuinely sorry for his mate: awful shame, that bastard Rymer finding out that Mac had financial interests in Mungana mines. Theodore eased his neck inside the stiff collar and wondered how long it would take for his own involvement to surface. He addressed the state organiser: 'Well, Joe, it looks like we can't afford the luxury of long-term plans. We've got to deal with the ARU now. It's no longer enough to force them out of the Party; we've got to make sure they sink. We'll continue to tread on eggshells as long as they have influence over railway workers.'

'I know that Ted, so does John here,' he said turning to Hayes. 'That's why you brought us the paper, right John?'

Hayes nodded.

A gust of wind threw heavy raindrops into the face of McCormack, still standing by the open window. He pulled the window closed and, with two deep creases between his eyebrows and thin lips curved downward, turned to Hayes.

'You're prepared to go to the papers with a story?'

Hayes pulled a sheet of paper from his pocket and handed it to the Premier.

'Already written the draft.'

Summer rain pelted against the window, and the reflection on the glass cabinet grew dim with the darkening sky.

Collings outlined his revised plan to the other men in the room: 'As John says, he's prepared to go to the papers. They'll lap it up. Nothing like a scandal within a union to get the presses rolling. He'll say that the ARU's Executive altered the minutes to save face and therefore can't be trusted. Coming from one of their own, it'll carry more weight.'

Hayes took up the explanation: 'Once I've spread the muck over Moroney and Rymer, I'll convince the boys to leave their union. They know you're setting up a railway branch in the AWU; what they don't know yet is that I'll be heading it.'

'Best keep that under your hat for now,' said McCormack, 'don't want to scare them off. You just make sure it looks like you're being forthright and trying to protect the interests of the rank and file.'

'There's one more thing,' said Collings. 'We need to deal with O'Leary. He has too much influence over the Annerley branch, telling them not to sign the pledge, even though he came to heel for the plebiscite. I don't think he'll leave the party of his own accord. It'll take stronger measures.'

Theodore said: 'I'm sure you'll find ways of dealing with him, Joe'.

He waved a hand of dismissal towards Hayes: 'Off you go, John. We'll see you right for this, but make it good.'

McCormack, Theodore and Collings watched as Hayes left the office.

Theodore collected his hat and cane from the coat stand: 'Don't particularly like that chap, but we can make use of him. He's hungry for power.'

Theodore stepped out onto George Street. The cloudburst had passed, leaving a damp and musty smell rising from the shiny black street. He headed to the Gardens for tea and quiet contemplation.

‏؞‏

John Hayes passed the point of no return when he called a special meeting of the South-eastern District on 26 February which, despite listening to George's justification of his actions for a couple of hours, carried the following resolution from Hayes:

> As this meeting is of the opinion that State Council directed ARU Convention delegates to sign the anti-Communist pledge without any qualification, it requests a special meeting of State Council be called to deal with those responsible for taking action to the contrary, thereby disfranchising 11,000 members of the ARU, placing them outside the ALP.

George had left the meeting, knowing nothing he could say would change the situation, and called the State Council to meet in a fortnight hence.

Without seeking ratification from his district committee, John Hayes declared his hand by presenting his press release to *The*

Daily Standard, accusing Tim of falsifying the minutes of January Council in order to save face after being refused entry to the Labor-in-Politics Convention.

Having now made his choice, John Hayes did not return to his office in the ARU rooms at Trades Hall.

෨

The printing press clacked and rumbled to its own rhythm, applying ink thinned by the Brisbane February heat. An ink-stained cloth hung from the bib of the overalls of the stout man watching over the printing. Fred Cook took pride in the relentlessness of the clattering press: it signalled to passers-by that Swift Printing Company was holding its own in Brisbane, despite competition from larger firms.

He turned at a sound from the office in the front of the building and walked through the internal door, wiping his fingertips on the dangling corner of the cloth. A sheet of paper fluttered on the desk as a motorcar drew from the kerb. With almost-clean fingers, Fred grasped the corner of the paper and pushed his frameless glasses up his round nose until the words *Red Rymer: A.R.U. Methods* came into focus. Above the words appeared the letterhead: Lippencott Co., Proprietor of *Mirror Newspapers.*

Fred sank onto the wooden office chair, for once forgetting to spread a newspaper beneath his inky overalls, and read the article. The rhythm of the presses changed and a man, taller than Fred, but clothed in matching overalls, appeared at the internal door to the office.

'What've you got there, Fred?'

Fred wished he hadn't seen the article first. Jim Hardcastle wiped his fingertips on his own dangling cloth and took the paper from Fred's extended hand. Fred wiped his fingers again, as if removing the print he had just read. He walked into the printing room and collected the freshly run sheets.

'Bloody hell!' came from the office. 'We can't print this! It's libellous.'

Fred continued gathering the freshly printed sheets.

'Send it back and tell him we're not prepared to print it.'

The next day Waller, principal of Lippencotts, entered the premises of Swift Publishers and pushed the article across the desktop towards Jim who was preparing the accounts for the end-of-month mail out.

'It is most important that this article appear on the front page of the next *Mirror.*'

'I'm sorry Mr Waller, but it can't be published, we'd be sued. And besides, we will not publish it because Rymer's a decent bloke.'

'You must print it. It's a big coup, and it means a lot of money to us, in fact, we've got a number of articles ready. McCormack has offered £100 a week while we publish them, but I need to have the galley proofs when I see him on Friday.'

Jim got up from the desk to summon Fred from the printing room.

'Mr Waller's brought the article back; says we've got to print it, but I said we can't.'

'No way, Rymer's a clean fighter, and we wouldn't do this to him.'

'I don't care whether Rymer's a clean fighter,' Waller replied. 'We are on the side where the most cash is.'

'Where did you get this information, anyway?'

'I interviewed John Hayes; and let me tell you, he's a bloke with inside knowledge. He's district secretary with the union. He was there when the vote was taken.'

'But to accuse the executive of falsifying the minutes! We can't take responsibility for printing that,' said Jim.

'You can, and you have to, or we won't get our cash. Next week's article's already written: *Who Audits the Railway Advocate's Books?*, Waller chuckled. 'I thought up the headline myself.'

'I'm sorry sir,' said Jim, 'but the matter's closed. We absolutely refuse to publish the article.'

Jim and Fred left the office and returned to the printing room.

But the matter wasn't closed.

One evening soon afterwards the two printers were running the *Mirror* when a car pulled up outside the office and four men entered the printing room, filling it with threat.

One of the men - Jarvis, Waller called him - stood over the press: 'Nice bit of equipment you've got here Mr Hardcastle. Be a pity to see it ruined.'

Jim ignored him and turned to Waller: 'Look, I've told you our decision'.

'And I've told you - I have to meet McCormack with another bloke on Friday, and unless we have the galley proofs, we will not be able to lift any cash. Anyway, I don't see what your problem is; I own the bloody paper - and a good paper it is too, a nice little earner for you. If anyone'll get sued, it's me.'

'But the *Mirror's* not a political paper. It's for the sporting fraternity! Why don't you try some other printer.'

'It's been refused in several quarters, but we *will* get it published.'

Waller turned to leave, and the other three men followed. At the door, he turned for one last word: 'I think it's time we took the paper from you and handed the printing over to Brookes'.

'Right!' yelled Jim. 'You do that. Take the paper away. We don't want it if it prints this kind of tripe.'

As the front door closed, Jim realised the offending article was still on the desk. He picked it up: 'I'll be late in tomorrow, Fred. I'll be paying a visit to George Rymer'.

'I'm coming too.'

☙

George arrived unannounced at the O'Leary home the following evening. This was not unusual as George lived in the next suburb and frequently dropped in to share a cuppa and an exchange of ideas.

Jack and Mary had finished dinner and cleared away the dishes for a game of cribbage when they heard a rap at the open front door.

'Hello! You there, Jack?'

'In the kitchen, George. Come through.'

Mary picked up her knitting: her way of being present without appearing to eavesdrop.

'We've got trouble, Jack. I had a visit today from Hardcastle and Cook, who print the *Mirror*. Apparently Waller came to them with an article which he wants printed on the front page, but they've refused to do it. Don't want to malign me.'

'Good to know *someone's* on our side. Did he say where he got it from?'

'Waller said he had inside information from Hayes.'

'What's in it for Waller?'

George told Jack the whole story.

The two men sat in silence, George sucking on a pipe, Jack on a cigarette. George removed his pipe and broke the silence: 'I must say it surprises me that Hayes has proved to be a turncoat. He's always put the union first.'

'He can sniff the power. Do you know what I reckon, George? I reckon McCormack got to Hayes. Just wait, betcha he'll end up as organiser of the AWU railways branch. Jesus, they go to a lot of trouble to manipulate the scene, don't they?'

Mary had been knitting quietly through all this, until now.

'What John Hayes's saying is not true! I was there at the Council meeting. I heard Mr McLary say the words 'under protest' when he moved the motion.'

'Of course he did, Mary,' said George. 'We all know that, but we can't prove it.'

George pensively stroked his moustache: 'The other day I was at Parliament House and I bumped into Bill Kelso. He said he's checked the companies' register and found McCormack has shares in Mungana. He's sent a letter to the *Telegraph*, and asked if I'd publish it in *The Advocate* too. Of course, I said yes. McCormack's a worried man right now, and that makes him dangerous. He's putting up a smokescreen, hoping the papers'll be more interested in the story of our union's supposed "fake" minutes than his own corruption.'

'I guess we can safely leave it to Kelso and the rest of the Tories to pursue that one,' said Jack. 'So what happens now?'

'We meet tomorrow for a special sitting of Council. I've asked Hardcastle and Cook to attend so they can put their case. I've also arranged for a shorthand typist to be present to record their submission, word for word.'

'Wise move.'

'I've interrupted your evening long enough. Sorry Mary, but I needed to chew the fat with someone.'

'That's okay George, you know you're welcome anytime.'

As the two men walked down the hallway, Mary heard George say: 'There's little doubt this'll cause a split, Jack. I know we've got your support, but you may have to think about your position in the union. You're too good a man to just be helping from the sidelines. The time'll soon come when you'll have to give up the workshop and come on board full-time.'

'Believe me George, nothing would make me happier.'

༄

'Stop scratching!'

Frank reluctantly pulled his hand from his neck.

'It'll never get better if you keep at it.'

Frank stared at the river, trying to ignore the burning itch. Gwen regretted her words as soon as they left her mouth and she playfully pulled Frank on top of her. Long grass tickled the back of her bare legs. Tiny black ants crawled between her toes.

'It'll be better before the wedding. Promise,' said Frank.

Gwen stretched her left hand beyond Frank's back, rotating her fingers so that the tiny diamond glinted in the sun's rays. Frank kissed his fiancé, drawing her attention away from the tangible proof of their betrothal.

They lay in the grass beside the Brisbane River, screened by the old willow that dipped towards the water. They had walked almost as far as the Regatta Hotel before finding a private spot. From beyond the tree came the clopping of horses hauling carts, and the occasional bleating of motorcar horns on River Road.* Very few pedestrians passed along this section of the overgrown track.

As the sun lowered behind One Tree Hill in the west, Gwen stood and shook grass seeds and creases from her skirt. Frank lay on his back with his hands beneath his head, chewing on a plump stem of grass, watching as she pushed her feet into her shoes and smoothed her hair.

'I'd better be getting home, or Mum'll be asking questions.' Gwen held out her hands and pulled Frank from the long grass that had hidden their lovemaking. They walked arm in arm along the river bank, in contented silence, and parted when they reached Victoria Bridge.

Gwen hurried along Ann Street to catch the next tram heading for New Farm. She hadn't meant to stay so long with Frank, and it was nearly evening when she climbed the front steps of her mother's cottage. She removed the ring and buried it deep in the pocket of her skirt before opening the door. Gladys was taking roast mutton from the oven when she heard the front door close.

'Where yer been, girl? What time do you call this?'

'I've been window shopping Ma.'

'Bloody likely! Hope you haven't been with that no-good Ryan. Nothing'll come of keeping company with him.'

* Now known as Coronation Drive

Gwen ignored her mother and went to the bedroom they shared. She slid the ring beneath her pillow, away from Gladys's prying eyes, and returned to the kitchen table.

෨

After leaving Gwen, Frank turned back towards the river. He squeezed between a picket fence and the concrete approaches to Victoria Bridge and clambered down the bank. In the dimness beneath the bridge, orange flames flickered brightly behind rusty holes in a forty-four gallon drum. Five rugged, ruddy faces encircled the smoky fire, absorbing its warmth, chuckling at a joke that hung in the air. A tram rumbled rhythmically above. Frank upended a wooden crate and pulled it into the circle.

'Gidday Frank,' said a dark-skinned young man. 'Ain't you got a home to go to?'

Frank smiled hello to Joe Esler. They had been bashing around together since school, but now that Frank had found himself a job and could afford a room in a boarding house, he rarely returned to their old haunt under the bridge. Frank engaged the circle of men in conversation, sharing new jokes he had heard at the brewery, passing around a cigarette packet, flicking butts into the flames. Eventually, he said to Joe: 'Fancy a pie?'

One of the other men looked towards Frank with expectation in his rheumy eyes. 'Not you, grandpa!' Frank said. 'I need someone who can stay upright.'

The old man snorted at the fire.

Frank turned to Joe. He had a use for his mate's skill with his fists; Joe could still swing an effective punch, even though it had been three years since he saw the inside of a ring. The two young men walked from under the bridge and climbed the riverbank onto the city streets, hidden beneath the cloak of darkness. They crossed the road to where a horse stood with its head drooped in sleep between two shafts. Each evening, that horse slept in his harness by the roadside from six o'clock until the early hours of the next morning when Fred, the pie man, hauled up the counter flaps of his pie cart and flicked his reins to head for home.

Frank approached the counter: 'Gidday Fred'.

'Hello young Frank. How's you been. Haven't seen you around for a while.'

Frank only ate at the pie cart when he was broke. Ever cheerful, Fred never refused a feed to anyone, drunk or sober, poor or not so poor. He kept a running tally in his head and often 'forgot' debts.

'Got me a job loading kegs at the brewery.' Frank flexed his biceps: 'Keeps me fit'.

'So, Frank, what'll it be?' With a tea towel, Fred mopped up gravy puddles from a previous customer.

'Pie and gravy for me and me mate, thanks Fred. May as well throw in a cuppa too.'

'What about peas?' asked Joe.

'Not bloody likely! That's another tuppence.'

Fred placed the pies on two large plates, ladled a generous amount of thick brown gravy over them, and rested knives and forks along the side. From a large enamelled teapot, he filled two chunky cups and placed them beside the pies. Frank dropped two shillings in Fred's fleshy palm.

They hoed into the meal, dribbling congealed gravy down their chins and shirts, and making small talk with Fred. When they had drained the cups and spat out the tealeaves, they wandered off down the road.

'Want to earn a few quid?' Frank asked Joe. 'It'll probably go on for a few nights, if you're up for it.'

'I'd be a mug to knock it back. When's it on?'

'Starting tonight.'

They turned right at the intersection into Turbot Street. Away from the centre of town with its lit shop windows, they walked unseen, except when they passed beneath the occasional street lamp.

'Who are we after?' asked Joe although, in truth, he didn't care so long as he got his money. He'd lived on the streets for so long he'd forgotten what a bed felt like, unlike Frank who drifted in and out of homelessness as often as he drifted in and out of prison.

'Anyone in the ARU,' replied Frank. 'Doesn't matter who, so long as we let them know they're being watched.'

As they crossed Roma Street, delivery carts and trucks were beginning to pull up to the markets, unloading sacks of potatoes, mountains of cabbages and tomatoes, fruit and vegetables ready for the sales that began at dawn each day.

'Guess what,' said Frank.

Joe didn't like playing Frank's guessing games.

'What?' he mumbled.

'Me and Gwen are getting hitched.'

'Yeah?' Joe was genuinely surprised. 'Does her old ma know that?'

'No, not yet. I just popped the question this afternoon. Should have seen her eyes when I give her the ring.'

'Where'd you get money for a ring?' Joe could not hide the sarcasm.

'Ask no questions...' replied Frank.

'Nicked it, eh?'

Frank ignored the remark, and lengthened his stride. He had bought it from a fence he knew, but it was none of Joe's business.

'Come on. We'll miss them if we dawdle.'

Leaving the buzz of the markets and the shunting of goods carriages in the railway yards opposite, they hurried on to Edward Street and turned left towards Trades Hall.

Waiting always made Frank's rash itch. He plunged his fists into his pockets and concentrated on the arched doorway lit from within the building. They noted a lean man with auburn hair descend the stairs, followed by a small man with a thick black moustache. Frank extended his arm and pushed Joe back into the shadow of the granite plinth of a monument on the footpath.

'The short one's Rymer. Don't know who the other one is, but we may as well get 'em both,' Frank whispered in Joe's ear.

Frank and Joe remained beyond the reach of the light until the two men had passed. They followed for two blocks along Edward Street, picking up the murmur of their voices without hearing the details of their conversation. As they approached Queen Street, the number of pedestrians increased, but this did not bother Frank; a laneway beyond the AMP building would give them the privacy they needed. He sped up, nodding Joe on beside him, and as George Rymer and Jack O'Leary reached the end of the laneway, Frank and Joe dragged them into the blackness between two buildings. Caught off guard, George and Jack felt the full force of half a dozen punches to their heads before they rallied and fought back. Jack split Frank's lip while George struck Joe on his ear. Frank yelled: 'That's enough!' and he and Joe ran along the lane and disappeared around the corner near the post office.

'You all right?' George helped Jack to his feet, feeling blood trickling down his own neck.

'Nothing's broken, as far as I know,' replied Jack. 'Should we call the cops?'

'No point. They won't be able to catch the bastards.'

George spat a gob of bloody mucous onto the footpath.

'Come on. I think we should get a cab home, we wouldn't look too good getting on a tram.'

Mary was sitting in the lounge, listening to the wireless, when a bloodied Jack walked down the hallway.

☙

Chapter 7 - Watch your back (1926)

March 14th, 1926

Dear Comrade Hayes,

At to-day's session of the special Council meeting convened to deal with your allegations regarding the minutes of the last State Council meeting, the following resolution was carried:- 'that in view of the serious charges covering minutes of last Council meeting, and also other statements made to meetings and press by District Secretary Hayes against the State Executive officers and council, and the evidence tendered to this meeting of his alleged conspiracy with certain other people in attacks on the State President and the ARU, this Council is of opinion that Mr. Hayes has forfeited its confidence, and decides that he be suspended forthwith and called upon to show cause to this Council meeting why his services with the union should not be terminated.'

I am directed to notify you that you are hereby suspended, and to instruct you to attend to-morrow (Monday, 15th instant) morning's session of the special Council meeting at 11 am.

Yours faithfully

Tim Moroney

State Secretary

Australian Railways Union

This is not what Hayes had expected from the State Council session. Unaware of the evidence given by Hardcastle and Cook on the first day of sitting, he had assumed Council was called to deal with his charges against Moroney and Rymer.

But after hearing submissions from both sides over three days, Council confirmed Hayes's dismissal, subject to ratification at a special conference called for a couple of months hence.

As soon as Hayes heard Council's decision, he rushed to *The Daily Standard* with an announcement:

A meeting of rank and file members of the ARU is called for next Sunday at the Stadium.

Three hundred and fifty railway workers ducked through the wicket door on the corner of Albert and Charlotte Streets and entered the cavernous amphitheatre to hear what Hayes had to say.

George and Jack attended the meeting along with Ted Foley, who had taken on Hayes' role as district organiser, but it was obvious from the outset that most of the workers, who had not been privy to the machinations of the executive, supported Hayes. They responded as any worker would on hearing of wrongful dismissal: they declared the position black and called for his reinstatement as district secretary. The three union men left the Stadium to resounding jeers.

Each day the papers feasted on this controversy. Hayes' vitriol knew no bounds, though his terminology was sometimes suspect:

Mr Rymer, like a carrion over the body of a dead beast, he swoops down, and, with poisonous talons, clutches a piece of the rotting carcass, gulping it down that it may supply renewed energy for further swoops and further gulps.

Back and forth went the letters between the *Standard* and *The Advocate*. And the *Telegraph*, preparing for its anti-Labor barrage with the state elections due in May, made much of McCormack's alleged connection with Mungana Mines.

Mary saw little of Jack during this month. There were so many meetings: branches, sub-branches, committees.

But George had a plan. Within a few days he needed to leave for north Queensland on an extended union trip. The district committee appointed Ted Foley as acting president during his absence, thus leaving the black secretaryship vacant. George asked Jack to chair a two-day meeting in April. During that meeting, Jack was seconded to the position of acting district secretary of the South-eastern District - as soon as he organised three months leave without pay from the Woolloongabba Goods Yards.

John Hayes, a convincing orator when his blood was up, travelled to every railway shed and maintenance gang in south-east Queensland during the month of March, whipping up sympathy for his position. The rank and file, trusting their district organiser, crowded the lunchtime meetings to hear his side of the story. Each face, grimy from the morning's work, soured with disgust as Hayes spoke of the union's executive sitting at their desks in clean clothes, making rules the railwaymen were expected to obey without question.

The cream silk of the shirt snagged on Jack's calloused fingers as, with guilty pleasure, his palms slid easily over the fabric. He closed his eyes. Such sensuous material belonged on a woman's body.

He lifted a pair of blue trousers from the bed and pulled the left leg over his foot, then the right. Again, the callouses tugged at the fabric, this time, fine wool. He buttoned the waistband, then the flies; slowly, deliberately, feeling the touch of silk and wool where he was more accustomed to gaberdine and flannel.

Turning to Mary he posed, arms akimbo, and awaited her praise. She smiled from the doorway.

'That's more like what a union official should look like.'

Jack revelled in his new position, though it was only temporary. His whole demeanour changed in those two weeks and

Mary knew he would never return to the railway workshops. He took care with his appearance, dressing in a suit and donning his hat for the train trip to the office in Trades Hall where he toiled at his task of preparing for the forthcoming union conference to be held in Townsville.

Each evening after work he spread *The Daily Standard* on the kitchen table, upon which he laid cigarette papers next to a pile of Town Talk tobacco and rolled a supply of cigarettes for the following day. When he had filled his silver cigarette case, he retired to his study to read until dinnertime. Reclining in a Morris chair, which he'd built on the workbench under the house, and surrounded by bookshelves, Jack lost himself in his private world. Every inch of the walls not occupied by door or window contained books. Serious books. Everything from *The Labor Law in Queensland* to Haeckel's *Evolution of Man* - and not one of them unread.

As for Mary, she found being a union official's wife more to her taste than being a wagon builder's assistant's wife. Life started to move at a different pace. They played tennis on Saturday, and on Sunday caught the tram to the city for a picnic in the Botanical Gardens.

But the novelty of their new life lasted just two weeks.

Illuminated by a full moon, *Fleurs-de-lis* danced on the cotton curtain as it moved with a soft breeze. Jack loosened his foot from the sheet to catch the cool air. Beyond the closed door, three quarters of the Westminster chimes rolled through the house, disturbing its silence.

'Quarter to what?'

It was unusual for Jack to stir through the night - something had woken him. He raised his head to listen, but the only sound was the slow breathing of Mary curled in deep sleep beside him.

A short while later the clock chimed two and Jack heard shuffling footsteps on the verandah. Mary sat up, wide-awake.

'What was that?'

'I don't know,' Jack whispered. 'You stay here, I'll go check.'

Jack lifted the torch from the bedside table, slid the metal switch on the side. Nothing.

'Damn thing!'

He belted it on the heel of his palm and a sickly yellow glow filled the reflector, barely showing the floorboards in front of his feet. He pushed open the French doors leading onto the front verandah; heard the click of the garden gate closing; saw a shadowy figure flitting between the bushes on the footpath. He returned to the bedroom.

'Well! Did you see anything?'

'Someone was running up the street. It was probably just a kid out on a lark.'

Jack snuggled down and pulled the sheet over his shoulders. 'Remind me to get new batteries for the torch in the morning.'

With ears strained, heart thumping, he had no intention of returning to sleep, but he did drift off, for the next he knew the clock chimed five. Jack slipped out of bed and parted the curtains on the doors. As he watched, the end of a cigarette glowed in the yard. He burst out of the door just as the gate slammed shut. He returned to Mary, agitated.

'We need to talk. Wanta cuppa?'

Mary dragged herself from sleep.

'I'll get it,' she said, and groped for her chenille dressing gown. In the kitchen, she opened the door to the firebox and blew the coals to life. Mirrored in the round pebbles of her glasses, they spluttered, sparked, and a flame wrapped around the short log she placed on their warmth. She closed the door and pulled the kettle forward.

Jack signalled a serious conversation by reversing his chair and, with a cigarette dangling between thumb and index finger, lit end towards his palm, rested his tattooed forearms along the chair's curved back, waiting for Mary to join him at the table.

'How bad's this going to get, Jack?'

Perspiration beaded on Mary's forehead in the close warmth of the kitchen. She loosened the tie on her dressing gown and fanned her face with an open hand.

'They're only trying to frighten me off. I'm sure it won't turn nasty.'

'Yeah, but I know you, and you won't be frightened off!'

'They don't know that.' Jack drew on his cigarette. 'How's the tea?'

A piccaninny dawn glowed through the rose-coloured arctic glass of the kitchen window. Mary lifted the steel plate above the firebox and toasted some bread to go with the tea. Not much point returning to bed now.

Jack scooped butter from the crock and spread it on the hot toast.

'Don't keep dinner for me tonight, I'll be late home,' he said.

'Again? The kids are starting to wonder if they even have a father.'

Jack kissed Mary on the top of her head - her fine blonde hair tickled his nose - and went to the bathroom off the kitchen to wash and change into work clothes.

Later, on his way to work, he stooped at the bottom of the front stairs to pick up a cigarette butt. He held it up to Mary, watching from the verandah: 'It's not one of mine'.

Jack closed the front gate and walked to Yeronga railway station. Mary's spine crawled at the confirmation of the night-time prowler as she walked inside and locked the front door. She jumped as a branch scratched across the tin roof.

The press stepped up its vitriol on the union executive, which now included Jack. The press also reported that victims of brutal bashings were found on the banks of the Brisbane River and in the dark alleyways between shops in the centre of town. All were supporters of the ARU executive.

Often, as Jack left his office of an evening, ghostly cigarette-smoking shapes trailed him until he caught the tram. Jack could not isolate his family from the repercussions of Hayes' dismissal, and midnight prowlers continued to rattle the O'Leary's verandah gate.

'Is this how we are to live the rest of our lives?' Mary asked after yet another sleepless night.

'No Mary. Of that I'm certain. They're waging this campaign trying to get the executive to reinstate Hayes. My guess is that once the Townsville conference is over - and I suspect Hayes' dismissal will be endorsed - his supporters will desert the union, and leave the rest of us to get on with our lives.'

The cleanup proved a messy affair. Hayes sent a series of sixteen-page pamphlets to all members of railway-related unions - the ARU as well as craft unions. This exercise cost money, somewhere in the vicinity of £440. Jack had no doubt that either the Premier or his lackey was financing the efforts of this now-unemployed man.

As Jack anticipated, the conference in Townsville ratified Council's expulsion of Hayes. When Hayes called a special meeting in Brisbane to object, only thirty men turned up. It appeared that finally the rank and file were beginning to see through the conspiracy against their leaders.

రా

'Lady Jane and Girofla have run out of ore.'

Across his Premier's desk McCormack, addressing Theodore, allowed the news of the desperate state of the Mungana mines the space it deserved.

'Bluff it out Mac, bluff it out. The only hard evidence they've got is that you own 388 shares in Mungana. Really, that's bugger all in the scheme of things.'

'But word is the Auditor-General's to make a detailed examination of the accounts, and the purchase notes and assays from Chillagoe,' the Premier said. 'How long do you think it'll take him to find out the government's actually *lost* £1,000,000 in the past six years?'

'That's not what the balance sheets say,' responded Theodore.

'No, but we both know they conceal the real position.'

'Look, in six months I'll be in federal parliament. It's guaranteed this time. Hang on till then, and I'll see things right.'

Theodore rose with his trademark confidence, flipped his hat onto his head and swung his cane.

'Cheer up Mac, nothing'll come of it.'

Jack's temporary position as district secretary stretched into months, and as he pushed the Hayes' controversy to the back of his mind, he began to find his duties intellectually fulfilling. He represented railway workers in appeals against Queensland Railway decisions, often winning the cases, and the O'Leary home life finally settled down. Jack endeavoured to spend time with Jackie only to find that his son - who had turned twelve - was already almost an adult and not interested in his father's company. In this, his final year of primary school, Jackie knew what he wanted from life: to be a journalist. He occupied every spare minute scribbling on scraps of paper, even on the back of dockets. Every piece of paper became precious. His room was out of bounds to everyone, including his mother.

One evening, Jack pushed *The Advocate* across the table towards Mary, with a cheeky grin: 'I suppose I'd better apply for that'.

Ad - AUSTRALIAN RAILWAYS UNION (Queensland Branch)

Applications are invited for the position of Organising-Secretary of the South-eastern District of the above-mentioned Union. Salary £8 per week. Election will be by ballot of the members of the District, and the successful candidate will hold office subject to the terms of the agreement entered into with the Union in accordance with Rule 24.

Applicants must have a general knowledge of railway working and be able to represent railwaymen at enquiries and Appeal Courts.

Applications must be accompanied by a statement of the activities and association of the applicant in the Labour Movement, and such statement must be supported by documentary evidence. Applications will close with the undersigned at 9am on September 20th, 1926.

W. METEYARD,

Room 44

Trades Hall, Brisbane.

'I'd say you had. After all we've been through since January.'

It struck Mary that the ad seemed to have been tailor-made for Jack. With the ballot ahead, Jack threw himself body and soul into his role as acting district secretary to prove he was up to the job; in the evenings, he sweated over his application. Each time he reached a final draft he screwed it up and started again. At 8.30 am on 20 September he handed his application to Bill Meteyard and went and got well and truly drunk after work.

Jack and Mary had to wait forty anxious days and nights before the results of the ballot were known. There were tense moments. Jack drank more than usual. They shouted at each other more than usual. Jack occupied himself writing letters to the newspapers and speaking at rallies.

There was trouble brewing in China: the Australian Government had sent six destroyers to China to protect foreign interests. Incensed that his own government was joining forces with other Imperialist governments against workers, Jack contacted various unions to drum up support for industrial action. He believed, along with many workers in Australia, that the Chinese were entitled to worldwide support in their efforts to obtain economic freedom.

He wrote a long article for *The Advocate* entitled 'The Trouble in China'. Before sending it off to be printed, he read it to Mary:

Is it because they fear that Britain, America and Japan will be overthrown by the Chinese? Not so. They are sent there to guard the interests of a few human 'sharks' who are sapping the lifeblood of the Chinese workers. China has always been the home of corruption and intrigue. There is never any shortage of tools and agents when money or positions are offering. This state of affairs always keeps one section of China at the other's throat.

'Can you say those things?' Mary interjected.

'I'm only stating the truth.'

He continued reading.

When Dr Sun Yet San became the leader of the Cantonese, he brought upon himself the hatred of Foreign Powers, owing to his organising the Chinese into a national organisation. From that time vested interests have been losing their grip, and have resorted to wholesale murder.

'Really? Murder!'

Jack peered over his writing pad, annoyed at having his flow interrupted again.

'Sorry. Go on.'

He cleared his throat, and continued:

One American was found drowned in the river. This was later proved to have been accidental, but a British captain demanded that the lives of two Chinamen be taken as a reprisal for the American who accidentally fell into the river.

Mary gasped. Jack continued reading.

Two men were brought on to the wharf, and slowly strangled to satisfy the lust for blood of an Imperialist officer. This brutal murder brought about a boycott of British goods and also the strike of the seamen.

'Oh Jack, how horrid. Did that really happen?'

'I'm afraid so.'

Pleased at Mary's reaction of horror, Jack read the rest of his article as she listened, appalled.

~

November came, and with it, the announcement in *The Advocate*:

O'LEARY WINS SECRETARYSHIP.

This came as no surprise. Altogether, six candidates had applied for the position. Jack's vote was double his nearest rival.

Jack was still theoretically on leave from the Gabba Goods Yards, and he wondered if he should apply for indefinite leave - in case things didn't work out. But when he approached Tom Rickard, who had risen to the post of supervisor, his mate showed him the door, saying: 'Be off with you, O'Leary. You'll be much more use to us as a union official. And good luck.'

☙

The only sound inside Trades Hall came from the scratching of the nib of George's fountain pen as he prepared the president's report for next month's *Advocate*. He was proud to be able to write that membership was on the increase.

George pulled the watch from his pocket. Eight o'clock. He screwed the cap on his pen and closed his notebook. If he didn't leave soon, he'd miss the last tram home.

He stepped from his office into the darkened hallway and met a stranger face to face - a huge man who dwarfed George.

'Who the hell are you!'

The stranger backed away, holding up both hands, palm outwards, asking: 'Are you with the ARU?'

'It depends. Who wants to know?'

'Me name's Jim Stone. I need to talk to someone from the union. I've got important information.'

George walked back into the union office and turned on the light: 'You'd better come in then'.

He sat down at his desk and nodded towards a chair against the wall. Jim pulled it up to the desk and leaned conspiratorially forwards.

George offered Jim a cigarette. 'By the way, I'm George Rymer.'

'Pleased to meet you, George. You put out *The Advocate*, don't you? I like to read that paper; it's the only honest one around today. I'm night watchman up at the Chillagoe Smelters. I got the sack last Friday because I stuck me nose in where it wasn't wanted.'

'Is this about McCormack?'

'Yep, and Theodore.'

'Maybe you'd better start from the beginning,' said George.

'I always keep m'self to m'self, but that don't mean I don't know what's been going on. Last Thursday, I overheard Goddard and Reid talking about how things're hotting up and they'd better get rid of the evidence. I opened me big mouth and said: "Is that what you keep your office door locked for?" That must've scared them. Next thing they give me the boot.

'At first I just felt real mad about the whole thing. Why should the bastards get away with it? I know - everyone knows - that Theodore and McCormack've had interests in the whole kit and caboodle for years, but you don't know who you can trust up there. Everyone seems to be under the influence of McCormack, he's such an arrogant sod.'

'You don't need to tell me that,' said George. 'Are you sure the evidence is there?'

'There's enough to give 'em both ten years in gaol!'

'Do you think you can get your hands on the proof?'

'I'd have to break in, but that won't be a problem. I'm pretty familiar with all the locks in the place. I'll have to be smart about it though; they're getting mighty jumpy. Reason I'm here: I wondered if you'd publish what I come up with.'

'I've got a better idea,' said George. 'I think you should hand everything over to Moore. He'll know the right time to expose it.'

'But he's leader of the Opposition! A Tory!'

'Tells you what desperate times we live in, doesn't it,' replied George. 'But we'll back you up in *The Advocate*. Even devote the whole front page of the next issue to it.'

'Yeah, great!' smiled Jim. Then he turned serious again: 'There's another problem. I spent all me dough coming down to Brisbane, I haven't got the fare back.'

George dug into his pocket.

'Here, let me know if you need more.'

'Thanks mate. I hate to ask.'

∾

In the far north-Queensland town of Chillagoe, Peter Goddard took advice from the Premier of Queensland and resigned as general manager of the State Smelters.

~

George and Jack were mulling over the details of Jack's forthcoming gang-to-gang organising trip when Miss Petfield tapped on the open door.

'A telegram, Mr Rymer.'

She placed a sheet of paper in his hands. It contained four words.

Got it! Jim Stone

The following week, the Leader of the Opposition dropped a bombshell by asking Parliament to order a Royal Commission into affairs at the Chillagoe Smelters and the Mungana Mines.

~

Chapter 8 - A traitor to his class (1926)

'Would you like to go on a holiday?' asked Jack as he folded a slice of bread in half and wiped the remaining gravy from his plate with little regard to Mary's obvious disapproval. Her grimace was tempered with surprise: they had never taken a family holiday.

'I wouldn't have thought you could, so soon after starting your new job?'

'George suggested it. He knows what a hell of a year we've had.'

The last time George had visited their home, Jack and Mary had been very short with each other. George obviously recognised the strain under which they'd been living.

Beachside scenes were conjured up by Mary's imagination: 'Where did you have in mind? I hear Southport is pleasant.'

'But you hate the beach! You'd burn to a crisp.'

'I could cover up. Anyway, it's good for the children to bathe in salt water.'

'What about the mountains?' he said.

'I'd rather the seaside.'

'I'd prefer the mountains,' interrupted Jackie, who, these days, seldom offered an opinion on family matters. 'All you can do at the beach is jump up and down as the waves try to knock you over; at least in the bush there are things to look at. And you can go for walks.'

'The boy talks sense, Mary,' said Jack, pleased for once to have his son agree with him.

'There's a village in the Blackall Ranges, goes by the name of Mapleton. It has a couple of boarding houses: one called Strongarra sends a bus to meet the train at Nambour.'

'And how do you know all this?'

'George told me about it a few weeks ago.'

Jack didn't tell Mary he had already made the booking.

Mary removed a bread-and-butter pudding from the oven and the smell of nutmeg rose through its crusty top to fill her nostrils. She placed it on a board in the centre of the table.

'We could walk through rainforests, you'd hardly ever see the sun, and being in the mountains, it's bound to be cooler than the seaside.'

Mary spooned the pudding into five bowls and handed them around the table. There was little point arguing for the seaside. 'So, when are you going to investigate it?'

Brown, blue and hazel eyes all keenly awaited the outcome of this tedious grown-up conversation.

'I'll look into it tomorrow.'

They all cheered.

≈

The holiday was an outstanding success: the train trip to Nambour; the clamber up the Blackall Range in the bus; the homely and spacious Strongarra with its wide verandahs and friendly owners all contributed to the excitement and complete change of scene the O'Learys so badly needed.

They played tennis on the court behind the guesthouse, walked in the rainforest and bathed naked in the freezing pool at the bottom of a waterfall, plucking fat leeches from their legs. Come New Year's Eve, Jack and Mary danced at the village hall. At midnight they sang 'Auld Lang Syne', and the pianist, tipped by Mary that the New Year also meant Jack's birthday, roused the entire hall to sing 'Happy Birthday' to Jack.

The family returned to Brisbane rejuvenated. Jack resumed his rounds of meetings and arbitration, only to find the turmoil in China had escalated and that the Australian government had taken for granted the co-operation of its workforce. At the January meeting of the South-eastern District Committee, Jack gave a lengthy address to a capacity crowd. During the following months many unions, concerned for fellow workers on the far side of the world, became involved in blocking the transportation of troops to China.

But Jack was restless. For much of his time at home, unable to shake free from the shadow of McCormack, he locked himself in his study writing articles for *The Advocate*. Upon hearing that the Premier had ordered unemployed members of the Building Trades Group to take the jobs of strikers or lose their sustenance payments, Jack wrote a letter spelling out how McCormack, by backing the Master Builders, had forced men back to work 'through hunger and want of their women and children':

> *The workers took McCormack from among themselves and placed him in parliament. He's ridden to opulence on their backs. Now he's off to London, and King George will probably ask him to dine. He'll wear a tall hat and spats; maybe he'll send the workers a photograph so they can admire his Apollo-like physique.*
>
> *But the future history of Queensland will show Premier McCormack as a political trickster, egoist and traitor to his class!*

☙

John Wren did not partake of business lunches: he preferred to make phone calls and, as much as possible, conduct his business away from inquisitive eyes. A small man who kept in good shape by walking everywhere on bandy legs - the legacy of a bungled attempt to set a broken bone in his youth - he spent most of his days behind his Melbourne desk, pulling the strings that kept businessmen and politicians dancing to his tune.

He tapped the fingers of his right hand rhythmically on the desktop and pressed the bell-shaped earpiece into his ear, waiting for his call to be answered. A click on the line interrupted the ringing: 'Mahony speaking'.

Wren ceased the drumming and, firmly grasping the candlestick mouthpiece, moved it closer to his lips. Wren did not announce himself over the phone: there was little need to do so, as his Collingwood vowels gave him away.

'Bill, I've been thinking about you. I reckon you're about due for retirement.'

'What makes you say that, Mr Wren? I've still got lots of go in me yet.'

'We wouldn't expect you to retire on nothing, now, Bill. There'd be something in it for you. Quite a nice something.'

'Well, put like that, I might have to give retirement some consideration.'

'You do that Bill. Get back to me when you've decided.'

Wren replaced the earpiece on its metal cradle. His steely-grey eyes lightened in satisfaction as another jigsaw piece was eased into place.

A fortnight later John Wren's own newspaper, *The Daily Mail*, headlined the news that William George Mahony, sitting member for the seat of Dalley since 1915, had decided the time had come to step down from politics. He sincerely hoped the brilliant Ted Theodore would see his way clear to stand for the ALP at the resultant by-election.

Ted Theodore was finally on his way to Canberra.

☙

Mary heard Jack come in the front door, and waited for him to enter the kitchen, place his gladstone bag on the table, and deliver a warm kiss to the back of her neck as he did each day. This evening, however, she was greeted by the words: 'I've got to go to Maryborough for a couple of weeks, love'.

Mary reached for another spud to peel and continued preparing the evening meal while she grappled with the notion of being without her husband yet again.

'Don't get in a huff, love. I have to go, it's my job.'

She delivered the cold silent treatment throughout the evening, answering in monosyllables, ignoring Jack's playful attempts to draw her from the dark mood. Her mood was no lighter when he left the house the following morning to catch a train north.

But Mary found that the O'Leary household functioned more smoothly when Jack wasn't there. The children seemed different, especially at mealtime. Instead of the constant deluge of politics and unions to the accompaniment of table thumping, the evening meal became a time of chatter about school activities.

Jackie had recently started at Commercial State High School near the Domain - an obvious choice for one intent on becoming a journalist. With his father absent, he acted every bit the young cockerel in the hen house. Mary found it easier to defer to him.

꩜

Jack arrived at Maryborough station late in the afternoon to be greeted by two men: Vic Wilson, the local union representative, and Lee Hickey who had recently been suspended from the railway workshops. A room had been booked for Jack at the Grande Hotel, two blocks from the railway station, so the three men walked to the hotel in the fading daylight.

'You'd better fill me in, Lee,' said Jack, settling in at the bar. Lee tilted his glass and drank half the beer before responding. He was young with a strong and honest face. 'I've been suspended.'

'What's their reason?' asked Jack.

'Well, officially, the Commissioner for Railways reckons there's no work for a plumber, and as the work I was doing was that of coppersmith and tinsmith, they've reclassified me as a tinsmith. I don't mind that so much, I get the same hours and the pay's the same, but I lose seniority; and I was hoping to be leading hand.'

'It's more complicated than that,' interrupted Vic, a solid man in his late forties. 'Some of the fitters who were looking to be smiths were overlooked, so they called a stop-work meeting to figure out what to do about it.'

'It's no secret that the Commissioner doesn't want me, or anyone else from the union, as leading hand,' said Lee. 'When I refused to move, the blokes declared the position black. It'll no doubt be taken on by a scab.'

'There's those in the local ALP who want to make life difficult. They hope us union blokes'll move on from Maryborough,' said Vic.

'It's not just in Maryborough,' said Jack. 'We're copping the same in Brisbane. But I guess you've heard about that.'

'Hayes? Oh yeah, we've all heard about that turncoat! He came up here trying to get us to leave the union, you know.'

When the publican called for last drinks at six, the three men climbed the stairs to Jack's room to continue their discussion well into the night.

In the morning Jack kicked two empty beer bottles under his bed and dipped his hands in the basin of water on the dressing table to rinse the fuzz from his brain. An hour later he turned up at the workshops freshly shaven and tidily dressed in his woollen suit.

He spent the day interviewing workers, detailing their comments and objections, gradually filling in the missing pieces in order to mount a strong case at the Appeals Board hearing the following week. At the end of the day a group of unionists retired to the bar of Jack's hotel. Each evening the group grew larger.

On Wednesday evening Vic said to Jack: 'You know Joe Collings is in town tonight?'

Jack gagged on his beer. 'Bloody hell, what for?'

'The local ALP branch invited him to give a talk. They reckon you haven't got the guts to show up.'

'Oh, haven't I! Where's the meeting!'

'Don't bother Jack, it's a set-up.'

'I don't care if it *is* a bloody set-up, I'm not going to be intimidated by the likes of Collings!'

'Thought you might say that. Come on, drink up and I'll take you there.'

Vic and Jack could hear the hum of heated debate half a block from the weatherboard hall. They entered through a side door into a sweaty room crammed with men on wooden forms who set up a chorus of 'Boo' as the two union men took their seats.

'You sure you want to stay?' asked Vic.

'Bloody oath,' replied Jack, strengthened by Dutch courage.

They listened as Joe Collings revisited the old ground of the John Hayes' affair, stirring the crowd to hatred of the union executive, ensuring that everyone realised Jack O'Leary, the scab who had taken on Hayes' black secretaryship, was in the hall.

Vic rose and pulled Jack to his feet.

'Come on. We've got nothing to prove staying here.'

They left the hall to jeers and hisses.

The next morning Jack returned to the workshops to resume the inquiry; but at lunchtime there was Collings addressing two hundred workers in the yard. The mood in the shed changed after that. No one wanted to talk to Jack about the case. So he took himself off to the pub again.

Jack was in no hurry to leave his room for the workshops the next morning. He'd been fighting a cold for weeks and each time he coughed, his head throbbed. He turned to the wall and drifted in and out of sleep, dreaming of knocks on his door.

'Jack. You in there?' It appeared it was no dream. He crawled from the bed, still not entirely sober from the previous evening's binge, and shuffled across the bare floorboards to open the door to the imposing presence of Tim Moroney.

'God! Look at you!' said Tim as he pushed into the room and closed the door after him. Jack stared at his boss, trying to comprehend why he should be in Maryborough, let alone in his hotel room.

'I've had complaints that Lee Hunt isn't getting fair representation. They reckon you've been drinking on the job.'

With that, Jack exploded to life.

'Be buggered I have! I've been trying to do my bit, but the whole shed's clammed up on me. I'm left to put the case together with whatever Lee can give me.'

Tim sat on the bed, pulled out his cigarette case and offered one to Jack who reached for it with a shaking hand. Tim crossed his legs and two empty beer bottles clattered out from beneath the bed.

'Pack your case, Jack, and get back to Brisbane. I'll take over from here.'

'Shit, Tim. You think I've been slacking off here?'

'It's not for me to say.'

Tim left the room and the silence enveloped Jack. Subdued, he returned to Brisbane.

'What happened? Didn't the enquiry go well?' asked Mary.

'It went okay.'

But she knew something was up.

From the time Jack began working in the city, Mary had met him for lunch on Fridays. It became her day in town. It was no coincidence that it was also payday. They both knew that the reason behind the weekly lunch was to ensure the pay packet did not arrive home by way of the pub, but they never discussed it.

On the Friday following Jack's return from Maryborough, Mary and four-year-old Hazel walked up the long hill to Trades Hall and took the lift to the union office. A young dark-haired woman with twinkling eyes greeted them at the front desk.

'Good morning, Mrs O'Leary.'

Hazel raised her arms, waiting to be lifted onto the counter. Miss Mulvihill unscrewed the top of the biscuit bottle, inviting Hazel to make her choice - a ritual they performed each Friday - before turning to Mary.

'Mr Rymer asked if you could drop in and see him for a moment. Hazel'll be right here with me, won't you?' Hazel nodded, mouth stuffed full of biscuit.

Mary knocked on George's door.

'Come in.'

He pulled a chair forward for Mary and perched on the corner of his desk, stroking his moustache as he always did in contemplation.

'Is something wrong, George?'

'Well, yes Mary.'

'It's Jack, isn't it? Something happened at Maryborough?'

'Tell me Mary - does he have a problem with drink?'

'No more than the next man. He sometimes comes home late and I know he's been drinking. Why? What's happened?'

'While Jack was in Maryborough I had an urgent telegram from the District Officers asking for Tim Moroney to go and take over the inquiry. Apparently Jack'd been drinking quite heavily and the District Officers claimed that Lee Hunt wasn't properly represented. When Tim arrived, he actually found that Lee didn't have any complaints against Jack's handling of the case, but there was no doubt he'd been drinking.'

Mary stared at her folded hands, embarrassed, not knowing what to say.

'I'll have to fully investigate the situation. I need to explain why a union official was not up to the mark while representing a member.'

'What do you want of me?' asked Mary.

'As State President, I need to investigate, and censure Jack if necessary. As your friend, I need to know if Jack has a problem.'

'If you mean, is he an alcoholic, the answer is no. I know he gets upset sometimes and drinks more than he should. That's always been his nature.'

'Well, perhaps we'll leave it at that, Mary. I don't mean to worry you, but I need to see the whole picture before the next State Council meeting.'

George walked to the door, and held it open for her, patting her shoulder as she passed.

Mary collected Hazel, now on her third biscuit, thanked Miss Mulvihill and walked through the office to Jack's door.

'Ready for lunch?'

He neatly stacked the papers he had been reading, and collected his hat from the hook on the back of his office door. They walked the block to Central Station Café in silence.

A well-presented waitress in a navy uniform led them to a table by a large picture window. The tables were dressed with linen cloths, serviettes and silver cutlery. Mary removed her gloves and adjusted her hatpin. The waitress poured two glasses of water and left them to study the menu.

Hazel knelt on the seat near the window, watching the trains puffing into the tunnel beneath as they pulled out from Central station.

'Jack, why did Mr Moroney have to go to Maryborough?'

Jack studied her intently.

'Have you been talking to George?'

'Yes. This morning.'

The waitress interrupted - pad and pencil poised.

'Are you ready to order, sir?'

Mary had lost her appetite, but couldn't pass the opportunity of a three-course meal for two shillings. They ordered the vegetable broth and roast mutton.

'Is this what'll happen when you're away from home? You'll get drunk?'

'That's unfair, Mary. You have no idea what happened.'

'No, but I'd like to know. Please tell me.'

'The first couple of days went well enough. I was on top of the situation, taking detailed statements from the workers involved in the stop-work. On the third day, one of the blokes said Joe Collings was in town.'

'Why was he there!'

'The union isn't popular with certain elements of the Maryborough Labor Party.'

Jack outlined his time at Maryborough, only pausing when the waitress brought their meals to the table.

'So, you're not an alcoholic, then?' Mary asked when they were alone again.

'Of course not! God Mary, what makes you say that? I just like a beer same as any other man.'

Hazel joined them at the table and they ate their meal in strained silence.

֍

During March George travelled to Maryborough to hold an inquiry into Jack's conduct. George's findings were that, while Jack was not drunk while conducting the initial inquiry, he'd been consuming alcohol during the hours he should have been at work. Council censured Jack, with the understanding that any recurrence would be dealt with severely.

The union held no grudges. In April Jack was appointed to a committee to approach all the workers in Queensland, through the Trades and Labour Council, to ask them to join the workers in

NSW in demanding an increase in the basic wage. They would also renew the argument for child endowment promised by the Labor Government for at least the past three state elections.

⌖

Voices, little more than whispers, bounced off the stone wall as women, some wives, some mothers, sat opposite their men in the visitors' room of Boggo Road Gaol.

Gwen repeatedly smoothed her hair, an action due more to nerves than any attempt at neatness, and averted her eyes from the names gouged into the surface of the pine table at which she sat. She started when the steel door to the visiting room slammed open and a guard entered, dwarfing the skinny prisoner before him.

Frank took the seat opposite Gwen, his face and neck red raw, and leaned back in his chair and began, with a fingernail, digging the morning's gruel from his teeth.

Gwen didn't bother with the formalities of greeting.

'You stupid, stupid bastard! Why did you have to go and get caught!'

It took every ounce of Gwen's self-control to stop from striking Frank. The rest of the visitors ignored her outburst; it was nothing new in that room. Frank shrugged. Words were superfluous.

Gwen removed the ring from her finger and threw it across the table. It clattered to rest near Frank's hand, but he didn't attempt to pick it up.

'I'm going back to Sydney. No use hanging round here. It'll be years before you're out.'

'Don't go on, Gwen. I ain't done nothing I haven't done dozens of times before.'

'Why'd you have to go and rob a judge's house, for crissake?'

'Thought it'd be good for a laugh.'

'I don't see you laughing now.'

Frank shrugged again: 'Anyway, it won't amount to much. I've got connections, you know.'

He pushed the ring back towards her.

'I wish you'd keep it, Gwennie. Nothing's changed. I still want to marry you when I get out.'

He nudged the ring closer. Gwen picked it up and replaced it on her finger.

'I'm still going back to Sydney, though, to get away from Ma. She keeps on at me about how you're no good. I can't stand the sound of her voice any more. Aunt Mildred says I can have me old job back at the laundry.'

Frank, unable to find the words to talk his fiancé out of leaving, returned to his cell with its toilet bucket in the corner.

❧

Chapter 9 - Gang-to-gang (1927)

In the steamy north Queensland town of South Johnstone, Andy Hynes crawled amongst the wheels that towered over his long wiry body, applying grease to the gears, checking the cogs for signs of wear. With crushing due to start in six weeks, Andy and the rest of the crew at the sugar mill had no spare time to discuss the transfer of the mill's ownership from the Queensland State Government to a local co-operative of cane growers - not until they were all paid off.

Andy, along with 1028 other hopefuls, applied for the 103 positions on offer, but he knew he wouldn't be one of those selected: not because of the odds, but because he was a unionist who spoke his mind and Gillian, manager of the newly-formed South Johnstone Sugar Milling Association, had used the opportunity to rid the mill of troublemakers.

When the 103 names were posted, it was obvious that 50 of the most active unionists had been replaced by men from outside the union. Andy approached Gillian demanding preference be given to workers from the previous seasons - as was the custom - but the new manager would hear none of it. Those workers who were members of the Australian Workers Union began picketing the mill in the hope of having the victimised workers reinstated.

In Brisbane, George Rymer kept an eye on the situation, wanting to avoid involvement (after all, his union felt little loyalty to the AWU, the union formed by McCormack and Theodore) but knowing that, if the strike escalated, they would be dragged into the dispute as all sugar was transported from the mill by rail.

☞

Jack set out on his first gang-to-gang trip as district organiser to speak, in person, to every railway worker in every railway station, refreshment room, navvy and fettler camp, goods yard, running shed, shunting yard and railway workshop in his district: to hear any grievances they may have; to rekindle their belief in the union; to remind them how, by banding together, they could improve their often-times miserable existence; to collect their union dues; and to answer their questions about their old district organiser, John Hayes. First stop was Gympie, where most of the men had resigned from the union in support of Hayes.

He arrived in Gympie mid-afternoon and went straight to his room in the hotel over the road from the station. From the upstairs verandah, he looked down on pairs of railway lines worn to a shine above rusted fishplates. The lines finally converged on the yard in a tangle unfathomable to the untrained eye.

He waited until the railway yards opposite showed signs of closing for the night. A loco shunted a carriage past points and disappeared into the carriage shed. The fireman pushed the lever, separating the lines again, and sauntered after his loco.

It was July, and the first westerlies of winter whipped along the verandah of the Railway Hotel. Jack turned up the collar of his overcoat and backed into the wind to shield the flame as match met cigarette paper. He drew deeply on the thin, hand-rolled cigarette until it burned evenly.

The last train from Brisbane slowed in a gush of steam into the iron-roofed Gympie station. Doors opened before it stopped completely and passengers poured from the carriages in a hurry to escape the wind and settle by their fireplaces. The stationmaster blew his whistle as the final door banged shut. The driver stabled his charge for the night, and the stationmaster locked the double door to his office and followed the engine to the shed.

Jack left the verandah to the wind and entered his bedroom, pulling the French doors behind him. He poured some water from the jug into a bowl on the dresser, dipped the pig's bristles of his brush and flicked off the excess, then dragged them through his hair. Obediently, it lay flat.

࿎

Fifteen years before, in this room, before this mirror, he had plucked a scarlet rose petal from Mary's fine blonde hair as she studied her reflection.

'It's strange, isn't it? I don't look any different.'

'Did you expect to, Mrs O'Leary?'

Mary laughed. 'When you say that, I feel different.'

She brushed her hair, prolonging preparation for their nuptial bed. Another petal fluttered to the floor. She bent to collect it and held it to her nostrils, slowly breathing in its musky perfume. Jack held her shoulders and gently turned her around to face him.

'I reckon we've waited long enough, Mary.'

࿎

Jack laid his brush on the dresser. His hair sprung free into fresh curls, and he formed deep waves across his head with his fingers, reflecting on how their lovemaking had progressed from that fumbling first night of their marriage.

The leather bag, filled with union tickets, weighed heavy on his shoulder as he stepped down the internal staircase with its worn floral carpet runner, and crossed the road to the railway yards. His nostrils twitched to the acrid smell of burnt coal and fine ash as he passed the ash pit. Until that moment, he hadn't realised he had missed the life of the yards, locked away as he was on level two of Trades Hall.

A dozen men perched on pumper trays or leant against a wall once painted green, but now stained black by coal-dust impregnated overalls. Each spoke with a cigarette stuck to his bottom lip.

Union organisers should wear a tie, polished leather shoes and a woollen overcoat, but in the presence of sweat-soaked gaberdine on men who have just stepped from the heat of the footplate, Jack knew he was inappropriately dressed. The grime from beneath his own fingernails had not yet faded with his office work.

'So, you're the bloke who's slipped in behind Hayes?'

Jack looked into the narrowed eyes of the speaker, unsure whether they belonged to friend or foe.

'I'm Jack O'Leary. I am now organiser of the South-eastern District, if that's what you mean.'

'Oh, we know your name, orright.'

Another man pushed off the wall with his elbow to stand upright: 'Hayes's been up here, telling us all about the union's exec. He didn't paint a pretty picture.'

'I'm sure he didn't,' said Jack. 'But don't you think you should hear both sides of the argument?'

The first man relaxed his shoulders.

'We'd like that, Mr O'Leary. I've been telling the blokes we shouldn't give up on the union until we find out why Hayes was shafted. I guess you're the one to tell us.'

'Bloody hell, what's with this "Mr O'Leary"!' said Jack. 'For crissake, I'm one of you. I was on the gang that built this bloody line! My name's JACK.'

'Well, why didn't you say so, Jack?'

The tension in the twelve men began to ease. Fettler and navvy blood flows thick, and so distrust turned to interest as they discussed the line that they all had in common.

An hour later, thirteen men crowded the narrow bar of the Railway Hotel and Jack's leather bag contained twelve paid-up union tickets. The first hurdle had been jumped.

The track inspector was waiting by his quad for his daily track run when Jack entered the yard at seven the next morning. Jack swung his kitbag onto the splintery deck and sat on the spare seat. Yesterday, after the meeting in the shed, he had arranged a lift the two miles to Monkland. From there he would walk the 25 miles of branch line to Brooloo.

Conversation was difficult over the roar of the engine and besides, the inspector needed to focus on the rail ahead. Years of sighting the left hand rail as it passed beneath the quad had sharpened his intuition, helping him to detect dips from washouts or wriggles from loose sleepers; so Jack settled into the bone-jarring seat.

At Monkland station, the track inspector stopped to let Jack off. Jack pulled the hemp rope tight through the eyelets at the top of his khaki kitbag, secured it to a metal ring at the bottom and slung it over his shoulder. He did not like the way it reminded him of the war, but the white stencil bearing his name, number, company - and his ownership by the AIF - was fading, and the kitbag was useful to carry the clothes he needed for the next three weeks. From his other shoulder dangled the union satchel with ticket book and propaganda leaflets.

He walked along the gravel bed between the rails, lengthening his stride to land on the wooden sleepers: sleepers he had laid. He knew every inch of the 25 miles stretching before him.

By sundown he'd walked six miles, stopping to talk with gangs on the line, and approached the fettlers' camp at Lagoon Pocket where he camped the night in an all-too-familiar 6ft x 6ft canvas tent. His legs ached, his shoulders ached, his head ached, but being back among the gangs, he felt comfortable.

He woke early the next morning, listened to the men preparing for their day's work, and remembered shivering his way along the partly laid track to days of pick, shovel and barrowing that had toughened his wiry body.

Jack farewelled the perway gang after breakfast and, hoisting his kitbag back onto his shoulder, walked to the next gang to renew old friendships and establish new ones. Three days and 25 miles later he arrived at Brooloo, the end of the line. He caught a train back to Gympie and booked in to the Railway Hotel again for the night.

The O'Leary household again slipped into an easy rhythm with just Mary and the three children. Between the words of Jack's letter from Gympie, Mary felt his pleasure at being back on the line. She read how Alice Johnson, now a mother of three girls, had unofficially become the 'camp mother'. She did not envy her that role. She smiled when Jack assured her he was keeping away from the grog; she frowned when he said he was developing a 'bit of a cold'.

From Gympie, Jack walked the second stage of his trip up to Theebine Junction, visiting all the gangs and station staff, then caught a train west to Kingaroy where sub-branch secretary Lafferty put him up for a night before showing him the ropes on the Kingaroy branch line.

It was exhausting. The tour covered two hundred miles, a large part of it on foot, and Jack could not shake the developing cold. However, support for the union increased as he spoke to the railway workers. Everyone wanted to know the inside story of the Hayes affair. Out on the gangs, they only got gossip, not hard facts. Hayes and his cronies had been through the depots and larger towns handing out their propaganda about George, Tim and the union. But the railway men and women were largely open-minded and sifted lies from fact.

Jack returned home after three weeks, his cold now developed into influenza. Mary saw the fever spots on his cheeks and sent him straight to bed. He did not object. Every limb ached. That night the bed shook constantly from his racking cough and the sheets became soaked from his hot body.

～

From deep below the surface of the earth comes the muted rumbling of falling rock. Five men - each black face indistinguishable from the other - stop picking at the coal seam and look back along the tunnel. From within one black face, the fourteen-year-old eyes of Jack O'Leary watch rock dust billow towards them.

'Run!'

But there is nowhere to run to.

The dust grows coarser and settles on the tunnel floor, covering one of the men. Rocks follow the dust, crunching his bones.

Water swirls dust into mud, rising to Jack's knees, his thighs. He floats upwards with it, past the faces of his companions, bubbles drift from their faces rinsed clean by the awful water.

Daylight.

Hands grasp at his slippery shoulders. Voices. 'Stay with us Jack. We'll get you out.'

'John! My name's John. John O'Brien!' Jack spits out black water with his words as his rescuers shake his shoulder, calling his name over and over.

'Jack, wake up!'

Bewildered, choking on spittle, Jack opened his eyes to meet Mary's. He sat bolt upright, unable to make sense of the walls around him. He started shaking.

'Are you okay, Jack? You were having a nightmare.'

He lay back, pressing his palms to his burning temples. Gradually his breathing slowed and he stopped shaking.

'Oh God, Mary. I was back down the mine. It was horrible.'

'You reckoned you were John O'Brien, Jack.'

'Did I? I can't think why.'

～

Upon hearing of Jack's condition, George asked the State Council to grant two weeks leave. The local doctor visited almost every day, but could do little for him. Mary cut up lemons and boiled them into a syrupy drink and made the Scotch broth her mother had fed to her when she was ill as a child. The children moved quietly around the house, speaking in whispers. Jackie occasionally stood at his father's doorway and asked: 'How's the old man going?'

When Jack finally emerged from the bedroom, he was so weak he could hardly walk. Normally trim, Jack now looked painfully thin.

On Saturday morning Jack lay dozing in his armchair, the sunlight casting crinkled mauve-coloured patterns across his face as it filtered through the closed window. He woke to the sound of a motorcar pulling up out front, an unusual sound in Venner Road in 1927. Filled with curiosity, Jack went to the front door to see George getting out from behind the wheel.

'My, aren't you flash!' Jack almost sounded envious.

Proudly, George stood by his new vehicle and removed a speck of dust from the nickelled radiator.

'I was just up the road and thought I'd call in.' His grin said he really wanted to show off to his friend.

Jack, still in his dressing gown, walked slowly around the vehicle. He ran his fingers over the outline of the badge on the radiator.

G-R-A-Y.

'It's built on a Holden body, and the upholstery is real leather,' George said as he leant inside, pointing out that it also had a speedometer, dash lamp and even a petrol gauge.

Mary joined them in the front yard, amused at the distorted reflection of her legs in the unblemished black paint.

'It must have cost a pretty penny,' said Jack - somewhat rudely Mary thought, but the question didn't bother George.

'£260.'

Jack whistled quietly through his lips, then started coughing as a breeze stirred.

'We'd better get you inside,' said Mary. 'Would you like a cuppa, George? I've just made a batch of griddle scones.'

Around the kitchen table, the talk stayed on motor vehicles for a while. But George hadn't been 'just passing'.

'I don't want to bother you while you're ill Jack, but we need you back in the office as soon as possible. The South Johnstone affair's about to explode. They're picketing the mill and management's getting nervous, asking for extra police to be sent to the district. I can't see how we can avoid getting involved if they declare the mill black.'

'It sounds as if I'd better get back to my post then.'

'I don't think you're well enough yet, Jack,' Mary said.

'As soon as you feel up to it, eh?' said George.

☙

- PART THREE -

After God had made the rattlesnake, the toad and the vampire, he had some awful substance left with which he made a 'Scab'.

Jack London

Chapter 10 - Strike! (1927)

Loaded cane trucks queued on the rails waiting to feed the idle conveyor belt. Crushing at the South Johnstone Mill should have been in full swing by now. Gillian, the new mill manager, approached the local growers to operate the crusher, and a few had turned up, but the farmers were wise: they knew that if they scabbed they would, in all likelihood, be black-banned in the future.

Day and night Andy Hynes and a growing number of workers, including Italians from the large camp at nearby Silkwood, picketed the entire district, intercepting men looking for employment at the mill, leaving them in no doubt as to the situation. The union went so far as to offer to pay their transport to Mackay, where they would be sure to find other work.

For many of the itinerant workers, English was a language they little understood, and heated arguments developed. Fists replaced words. People carried guns. Men, determined to enter the mill, found their positions declared black. Striking workers and wives of picketers brought food to the line. They were in for the long haul.

ও

Andy Hynes pulled a packet of cigarettes from his shirt pocket and bent his head towards the match in his hands at the precise moment the bullet entered his chest. The picket line froze, unable to comprehend the image of one of their number collapsing before them, then surged around this most likeable of unionists.

꩜

Acting-Premier William Forgan Smith dithered over decision-making, cursing his Premier's absence overseas - even if the trip was an attempt to prise money from hard-nosed financiers to help the government out of a tight spot. In the aftermath of the bothersome shooting of the picketer Hynes, he ordered all firearms in the South Johnstone area seized. That would make it look like he was in charge!

The AWU executive, opposed to direct action, tried time and again to settle the dispute through the Arbitration Court but the rank and file refused to work beside scabs. And there was another complication. The union's executive, loyal to Premier McCormack, feared the railways union would become involved once the storage facilities at the mill were exhausted.

The strikers formed a Disputes Committee to handle their own affairs and called on the Trades and Labour Council at Innisfail to declare black the mill and all sugar leaving it. The waterside workers at the port of Mourilyan upheld the ban, but the railwaymen were told to stay out of the strike.

Davidson, the Commissioner for Railways, accepted the consignment which would normally have been sent by ship, and ordered the railwaymen to transport the sugar to Brisbane. In Brisbane, Tim Moroney and George Rymer sent word to their northern members to refuse to touch the banned sugar.

Not all railwaymen were members of the ARU. Many engine drivers belonged to the Australian Federated Union of Locomotive Employees, headed by Theo Kissick. They distanced themselves from the radical ARU and were only too happy to drive the banned shipment south to Brisbane.

๛

'Someone's looking after you,' said the prison guard as he fitted the large iron key into the lock of the double cast-iron gates.

Frank Ryan ignored the guard, and his comment, and walked through the arched gateway without a backward glance at the 20ft high brick wall with its red and cream horizontal stripes, but the words *H.M. Prison for Men* burned into the back of his head. He wore the same clothes he had worn when he had been brought to Boggo Road. There were no extra possessions to carry under his arm in a brown paper bag.

He pulled the collar of his rough cotton shirt high against the cold wind whistling along Annerley Road and headed for the city. After three months of regular meals, his weedy frame carried a comfortable covering of flesh and the rash had all but disappeared due to regular bathing with caustic soap. His legs, programmed to walk in circles around the exercise yard, had difficulty adjusting to the straight three-mile walk. Crossing Victoria Bridge, he paused to watch boats belching black smoke as they passed beneath his feet. A man steering a dredge waved. Frank snorted at him.

As he neared the city side of the bridge he could smell smoke rising from the riverbank. He slipped through the gap in the picket fence and clambered down the bank. The same bodies were still sitting hunched around the forty-four gallon drum, as they had been when he last saw them.

But he noticed a change in the hierarchy. Joe now occupied his old position on the far side of the fire where a bloke could see the cops coming and could make a quick get-away along the riverbank. It had always been his possie. Joe saw Frank approaching and grinned, but did not rise or offer up his wooden crate.

'You're out early, ain't yer?'

Frank pulled an old rusted kerosene tin close to the fire. The same five heads, and the same five pairs of eyes, bleary from the day's White Lady metho, nodded then stared back at the fire.

'Let me out on good behaviour.'

'Oh yeah!' Joe doubted that.

'What's been going on, then?'

'There's a bit of work around,' said Joe. 'Usual stuff. Union bashing.'

'Any on tonight?'

'Could be.'

'I need a piss,' said Frank, and walked to the river's edge. He could not explain how good it felt peeing into the wide river instead of a twelve-inch galvanised bucket. His boots gave off a stench of stale urine.

～

Bill McCormack removed his hat and threw it across the room in the direction of his hatstand, not caring where it landed. His bulky frame had increased during his time in London.

He was trying to decide which crisis to address first when the shrill bell from the telephone caused him to jump. He listened to the voice in his ear, then yelled into the mouthpiece: 'Get over here right now, and bring Davidson and Larcombe with you!'

Ten minutes later Forgan Smith entered the Premier's office followed by Larcombe - the small, dapper, bow-tied Minister for Railways - and James Davidson, Commissioner for Railways.

McCormack waited until the men were seated in the leather chairs on the other side of his desk before saying: 'I want an explanation, and it'd better be good'.

As the most senior of the three, Forgan Smith attempted the explanation in his thick Scottish accent, something that had always been a source of annoyance to the Premier who understood little of what Forgan Smith said.

'We tried to contain the strike, but the bludgers won't play the game. They've refused everything the Arbitration Court has thrown at them. They say they'll only go back if the mill sacks those it's put on since the strike.'

McCormack turned to Davidson: 'Where do we stand with the railways?'

'The AFULE's on side. They'll haul what's at the mill for now. Unfortunately, the ARU are sticking their bib in and have told their members not to touch the stuff.'

Larcombe, who had been silently examining his fingernails, said: 'Keep directing the railwaymen back to work, Jim, we'll uphold your orders. So long as we can shift the sugar on from the mill, we should be able to localise the strike.'

'By God! You'd better be right,' thundered McCormack. 'The last thing we need right now is another state-wide strike involving the ARU.'

Alone again in his office, McCormack removed a manuscript from the top drawer of his desk and gave it his full attention: the Auditor-General's departmental enquiry report on Chillagoe could have far wider repercussions than a few mill hands not wanting to work beside scabs.

He leafed through the pages to grasp the direction of its content, and drew a breath of considerable relief to find he was barely mentioned. Beale had reported the loss of £1,164,822; but that was to be expected - it was part of the Terms of Reference he had carefully written for the Auditor-General to follow. Still, it was a pity that Fred Reid's preferential treatment by the smelters was exposed, but someone had to take the fall.

෴

By 29 August the strike at the South Johnstone Mill had escalated. In support of the striking mill workers, railwaymen refused to bring the cane from the growers to the mill, and Davidson suspended anyone who disobeyed his orders. Then, of course, the job of each suspended railwayman became black, which no self-respecting unionist would fill.

Coincidentally, that same week, George Rymer appeared before the Arbitration Court in an attempt to secure changes in the Railway Award for all Queensland railway workers.

Seizing on the opportunity to sidetrack the union's further involvement in the South Johnstone dispute, Justice Webb threatened to dismiss the claims if the union did not send their men back to work, but George and Tim would not ask their members to scab. Upon hearing of the dismissed claims, the AFULE, whose members would also have benefited from an increased award, withdrew their support for the Commissioner of Railways and threw their lot in with the strikers.

≈

The debate had been going for nine hours, and members on both sides of the House were growing weary with it. McCormack answered yet another question from the Opposition: 'With apologies to Minister Larcombe, I am personally taking control of the Railway Department from today. Further, as the Australian Railways Union have officially decided that orders from the Commissioner for Railways are to be disobeyed, and their members are complying with this decision, it has been decided to dispense with the services of all members of this union as from Saturday, 3rd September, at 12 noon. Their dismissal is subject to re-instatement upon signing a pledge to obey the Commissioner's instructions.'

This came as a complete surprise to Minister Larcombe, sitting in the front bench behind the Premier. He always considered himself in control; always had the words to express - most eloquently, he thought - his intentions. He looked up at his premier, dumbfounded.

From the gallery, John Hayes had watched the entire debate with keen interest. No longer a member of the Australian Railways Union, he was in the process of setting up a railways section within the Australian Workers Union. He knew that, bound by the Arbitration Act, the Premier could not legally single out any particular union as he had threatened; and anyway, the Railway Department did not keep on record such information as its workers' preferred union.

He caught up with McCormack as he left Chambers, explaining that, should the Premier proceed with his threat of sacking ARU members, he could be fined £50 for each of the 11,000 ARU members. Even McCormack considered this too high a price to pay to settle old scores.

So he did the next best thing. At 1.10 pm on Saturday 3 September, 18,874 Queensland railway workers, from station staff to the keepers of the manned railway gates, received an urgent telegram from the Commissioner for Railways:

> *It is necessary to dispense with the services of all employees and this is an intimation to each employee that his or her services are dispensed with as from noon on Saturday 3rd September 1927.*

George Rymer declared: 'This challenge will be accepted and fought to the bitter end'. ARU sub-branches unanimously supported their leader's stand, as did many ALP branches with militant union membership, which of course included the Annerley branch and its secretary, Jack O'Leary.

With the gloves now off, a state-wide strike quickly developed following the lockout. While McCormack sidestepped the unions, dictating directly to the strikers, the Disputes Committee met daily at the ARU office in Trades Hall. Represented by 17 different unions including the Australian Railways Union, the Australian Federated Union of Locomotive Employees and the Australian Workers Union, it was never going to be a harmonious group. Theo Kissick, from the AFULE, would have nothing to do with the various union reps and would only speak with the AWU. He went so far as to refuse to appear on the same platform as George and Tim, representing the ARU.

Incensed by a Labor Premier locking workers out of their place of employment, the entire trade union movement in Australia voiced its support for the mill workers and the railwaymen. Several Labor politicians let it be known they disagreed with their Premier.

The Labor press, which normally sided with the Labor Party, were sympathetic to the strike, publishing a half-page photograph taken from the back of the crowd and showing a sea of hats and suits:

> *It was estimated there were between 6,000 and 7,000 workers present at the great gathering of locked out railway and trade unionists which took place last Sunday afternoon in the Brisbane Domain.*

The large gathering had come to hear Fred Paterson who, upon hearing of the lockout, immediately contacted the ARU to offer his services. Despite now being Deputy Lord Mayor of Gladstone, Fred wasn't well off; even so, he paid a man to look after his pig farm for a fortnight while he gave his time freely to the locked-out workers.

Each day the all-too-familiar daily routine of marches, meetings at Trades Hall, the Domain and the Stadium, resumed in Brisbane. *The Advocate*, full of reports of 'McCormack and his Scabinet Henchmen', also reported of nightly bashings in the city streets.

It became obvious to everyone on the Disputes Committee that McCormack always appeared to be one step ahead of them. After one meeting at which the delegates thrashed out important strategies that could only be put into effect if they all agreed to the utmost secrecy, Tim noticed Kissick's quick departure from the meeting room and followed him: straight to McCormack's office.

Rowdy rank and file meetings highlighted the differing attitudes of the strikers. As McCormack had hoped, dedication to the cause began to wane. He put pressure on the Arbitration Court to threaten the Australian Workers Union with deregistration, cancellation of awards, and loss of preference for its members in the workplace, unless it accepted the terms offered. He gave the executive just 24 hours to make up its mind. The AWU, which had initiated the strike, agreed with the proviso that all railwaymen be reinstated without victimisation.

At midnight on 11 September, trains started rolling again in Queensland. The next day, striking mill workers at South Johnstone voted to return. Forced to work beside scab labour, however, they disrupted the mill for several months.

The extra police sent to the South Johnstone district returned to their usual beat after finding that no one in particular was responsible for the shooting of Andy Hynes. The files slipped to the bottom of the pile where they remained, unattended. His life and death faded from public view.

৵

McCormack's victory was hollow. Thirteen Labor politicians objected to his high-handed tactic during the dispute - actions that would have been considered extreme even for a Tory premier. Unable to isolate a couple of hundred ARU unionists in the South Johnstone area, he had brought the whole of the state to its knees. The entire labour movement criticised him. George stepped up his own condemnation of the Cabinet and personal attacks on the Premier in *The Advocate*:

Oppressor of the working class.

Tool of the Tory Press…

৵

As the year drew to a close, with numbers in his union beginning to increase but morale still low, Jack suggested holding a smoke social to honour Fred Paterson and show appreciation for his unselfish efforts during the strike. He immediately wrote to Fred and Lucy, inviting them to attend the event without letting on they were to be the guests of honour.

It had been years since Mary had a new dress, so she took advantage of the excuse to make one. She knew she looked good in her silk shift with glass beads sewn around the dropped waistline.

She and Jack caught the train to town and walked the well-trodden route up Edward Street to Trades Hall. The air was thick with smoke and conviviality as George welcomed them to the meeting room on the top floor.

'What a wonderful turnout!' said George. 'I bet there's not a railwayman who isn't here tonight. Fred and Mrs Paterson haven't arrived yet, though.'

'I expected them on the afternoon train from Gladstone,' replied Jack. 'Perhaps they've gone to their hotel to freshen up.'

'Perhaps.' George turned to Mary: 'Would you like a drink, Mary?'

'Just a cordial, thanks George.'

'What about you Jack? Shandy?'

He guided them to the drinks table.

At eight o'clock, Fred and Lucy still hadn't arrived.

Distracted, Jack circled the room searching for them.

'I can't understand what's keeping them,' he said to George.

'We've got to go ahead with the evening, everyone's waiting for the entertainment. I think we should make a start and hope they arrive before the presentation. You did send the letter, didn't you Jack?'

'Yes. Over a week ago. It should've only taken a couple of days at the most.'

George stood on the platform at the end of the room - hands raised above his head - and waited for the chatter to stop.

'Ladies and gentlemen. May I say how wonderful it is to see so many of you here tonight. This is indeed a fine display of unanimity. It's very welcome after such a divisive year. As you're all aware, we're gathered this evening to honour Comrade Fred Paterson who preaches the ideals of solidarity among the workers and is always ready to aid the cause of industrial unionism.'

Everyone clapped.

'I know you all want to thank him in person, so do I. I can't explain why he isn't here yet. I can only assume he's been held up on the journey.'

George proceeded to eulogise Fred for the next ten minutes.

'On behalf of all Comrade Paterson's admirers in all sections, I'd like to present him and Mrs Paterson with these gifts. I ask Comrade Jack O'Leary to come forward and receive them on their behalf.'

Jack accepted the two parcels and, placing them on the table, addressed the gathering.

'On behalf of Fred and Mrs Paterson, I thank everyone for coming here this evening. I'm sure he would be greatly humbled by your presence, as well as your presents. I'd personally like to say how I appreciate one such as Fred, a Rhodes scholar and Oxford graduate, placing the whole of his fine educational ability and natural talents at the disposal of railwaymen in their time of trouble. I will ensure Fred and Mrs Paterson receive these beautiful gifts as soon as possible. Ladies and gentlemen,' raising his glass, 'I give you Comrade Fred Paterson!'

'Comrade Fred Paterson!' Everyone drank his toast.

Jack rejoined Mary.

'What did they get?' she asked him.

'Fred got a suitcase, and I believe Mrs Paterson's is a dressing table set.'

While the speeches were rolling, Tim stepped onto the platform and proposed a toast to the Labour Movement: 'I regret that there are still people who think that the Labour Movement can be only associated with the pick and shovel work. The participation of men like Mr Paterson disproves this. No man can do justice to such a subject in the course of a brief address such as this.

Notwithstanding the betrayals of Bill Kidston, Bill Holman, Bill Hughes and Bill McCormack, the cause still goes marching on.'

'Best to dodge anyone called Bill,' Mary whispered in Jack's ear. He grinned.

Then someone toasted the Labour Press.

'Any excuse for a toast,' Mary thought.

Eventually, the speakers all left the platform and the evening was given over to a program of singing and recitation by various members of the Union. At eleven o'clock Jack stood on the platform and in his strong tenor voice, led the singing of 'The Red Flag'.

A bell rang to clear the hall, but hardly anyone took any notice. By then, the atmosphere was so thick it was difficult to breathe, but the alcohol made it a jolly gathering, and they all stayed on to the small hours of the morning.

George drove the O'Learys home, along with the gifts for the Patersons. As they finally lay down to sleep, the clock in the lounge room chimed half past two.

'What a pleasant evening,' Mary sighed, as she kissed Jack goodnight.

'Yes. Fred and Lucy would have enjoyed it.'

The next morning they both rose with headaches: Mary from the smoke; Jack from too many shandies.

On Monday Jack sent a telegram to the Patersons and forwarded the two parcels to Gladstone by train. On Friday he received a letter from Fred explaining their absence.

Blarney Point
Gladstone
Nov. 24 1927
Dear Jack,

I want you to convey to all Brisbane members the thanks of Mrs. Paterson and myself for the beautiful and useful presents which they have given to us.

The presents themselves are very welcome, but what is more pleasing is the fact that you have in the ARU members who not only stood the test of scab-manufacturer McCormack's bluff, but also appreciated the assistance which I was able to offer.

Tell your members that it was a great pleasure to help them and their officials in that fight against scabbery, and my reward was obtained when they were able to go back in a body with the union honour and the working-class principles of the ARU still intact, and even more widely recognised than before.

Today, the name of the ARU stands high among unionists and if ever the time comes again, and I am sure it will, when the ARU is faced with the alternative of constitutional scabbery or trades unionist action, then I will be ready to hop into the fray immediately.

Mrs. Paterson and I were very sorry that we were unable to attend the smoke concert, but the letter came too late to enable us to catch the train. The letter was actually six days on the way.

In conclusion, tell your members that The Advocate *is still coming to me, in spite of the petty, spiteful, and childish action of the Tory Scabinet of the ALP in withdrawing the privilege of free carriage hitherto accorded it. That action is the greatest compliment ever paid to* The Advocate.

Yours for the workers,

FRED. W. PATERSON.

≈

Chapter 11 - An ailing world (1927-1929)

Gwen Ryan adjusted the thin strap on her bony shoulder and smiled for the camera from the top step of the registry office. 'You look bonny, lass,' said her Aunt Mildred.

Frank looked at his bride as the shutter opened, capturing a look of intense pleasure that overrode his cocky demeanour. The wedding party consisted of just four people: bride, groom, bride's aunt and bride's uncle.

A fortnight after his release from gaol, Frank had made his way to Sydney - catching rides in trucks, jumping railway carriages and walking a good deal. He arrived at Aunt Mildred's home late one evening and knocked loudly on the front door, caring little that the household had retired. Alfred opened the door with Mildred peering over his shoulder.

'Is Gwen here?'

'Good lord, Frank! What do you mean by coming here at this hour? Aren't you supposed to be in gaol?'

Frank pushed past them and shouted into the darkened house: 'Gwen, you there?'

Through a bedroom doorway, suddenly flooded with light, walked Gwen, rubbing her eyes with the heel of her hand. 'Frank!' She stopped rubbing and her eyes focussed. 'You haven't escaped, have you?'

'Shit missus! Give us some credit. No, I've come to get you. We're getting hitched this week, whether you like it or not.'

Aunt Mildred pulled Alfred back to their bedroom: 'We'll leave the young-uns alone, Alf'.

A week later they were wed before the registrar without the mother-of-the-bride who would not have attended even if she had known. After the formalities, Mildred and Alfred shared dinner with the newly-weds at a not-too-fancy cafe: their wedding gift.

The next day Gwen arrived early for work in the ladies' department of Grace Brothers. No one saw her slip the pale pink taffeta dress back on the hanger and smooth down the creases.

ঞ

More About Mungana: Definite Charges Made in Parliament. The headlines slapped McCormack in the face.

In walking out of Parliament when the Deputy Leader of the Opposition began his lengthy speech, McCormack thought he had been spared the grubby details: but here they were, reproduced in minute detail on the front page of *The Advocate*: every word of the charges of his own involvement in Mungana.

He folded the paper inside *The Daily Standard* and glanced around the private lounge of the Bellevue Hotel. Most of the other parliamentarians were either engrossed in conversation or their own newspapers and hadn't noticed their Premier's discomfort.

The door swung open and in walked Joe Collings. McCormack watched as the state organiser removed his coat and hat and hung them on a row of hooks on the wall then smoothed his hair. It was something of a coincidence that Joe Silver Collings, named after his father, had a head of such fine silver hair. Most people mistakenly thought 'Silver' a nickname because of that hair.

Collings looked towards the chairs by the large window to find the Premier sitting in his usual position. As Collings crossed the carpet in small, mincing steps, McCormack laid the paper on his lap and thought how much he did not want this meeting to take place; but Collings was on the Central Executive, and his questions needed to be answered.

Collings sank into a capacious leather chair beside McCormack and took his time lighting a cigarette, revelling in this moment of power.

'Would you like a drink, Joe?' asked McCormack.

Collings nodded and drew on his cigarette.

McCormack returned from the private bar with a beer and lemonade. He did not know whether Collings was a tee-totaller from choice or necessity.

'It was a mistake to challenge Moore to lay specific charges, Mac. He's serious about a Royal Commission, claims you and Ted used your public positions for private gain, especially seeing you were part of the Mungana syndicate. And, of course, he won't let the Auditor-General's report pass without mention.'

'Beal's only implicated Reid,' replied McCormack. 'My name's in the clear there.'

'Still, it looks suspicious. Especially when you walked out of the House without even hearing the charges. But I think we've quelled the attack for now.'

Collings drank his lemonade in one prolonged gulp and wiped his top lip with thumb and forefinger. He continued: 'It was bloody lucky that the Auditor-General's report coincided with the South Johnstone mess. Are you sure you didn't make more out of that than you needed to? To push Beal's report into the background?'

McCormack just smiled.

'I wouldn't be smiling if I were you. You've seen this month's *Advocate*, I presume?'

McCormack did stop smiling. 'Don't worry about Rymer. We've got ways of stopping him.'

'I wouldn't be so sure, Mac. He's threatening to bring it all up at Convention.'

'It won't do him any good. We've got the numbers.'

'You'd better start preparing your answers to satisfy the rank and file. And while we're on the subject, what are you going to do about that night watchman, Stone? He reckons he's got incriminating evidence on you and Ted after breaking into Goddard's office.'

McCormack's veins stood out on his neck; his face turned bright red. 'Let him say that publicly and I'll institute an action for criminal libel against him and anyone else who defames me!'

'They'll use parliamentary privilege, and you won't be able to touch them,' replied Collings.

'I can't see what they can do. With Goddard's resignation, the smelters have closed down; that should put an end to the whole business. The worst they can do is prove that Goddard favoured Reid when it came to getting ore for the smelters. Goddard's prepared to take full responsibility for mismanagement. As for me: I was Home Secretary when the Government purchased Mungana Mines, and Speaker when they took over the smelters - quite outside politics. There was no conflict of interest.'

'I hope you're right about that, Mac. It wouldn't look good for the government to have its Premier accused of malfeasance.'

'No need to worry, Joe.'

❧

The Australian Railways Union began to claw back its strong position in 1928. Membership increased four-fold, thanks largely to Jack's zeal in the South-eastern District. Little by little he persuaded railwaymen to stay with the union and signed up an increasing number of new members each week, despite attempts by the Australian Workers Union to body-snatch members for their new railways branch under the leadership of John Hayes.

Jack's district stretched from the New South Wales border north to Maryborough, and kept him away from home for weeks at a time. When he was in Brisbane, meetings and office work consumed him. Mary admired his dedication, a quality that made him popular and respected across the Labour Movement, but this dedication came at the price of his role as father and husband.

While Jack was home, George visited often and the two men involved Mary in discussions on union business. While Jack was away from home, she had absolutely no contact with the union. She found it difficult to drop in and out of such a hot-house existence. Suggesting that a family holiday would make amends for Jack's neglect over the past few months, Mary announced, over an evening meal in February: 'This year, I'd like to try the seaside'.

'Why?' asked Jack. 'We had such a wonderful time at Mapleton.'

'There's no question about that. I just feel I may be missing out on something. I'd like to see what the seaside's like.'

Mary could taste the disappointment around the dinner table as everyone looked at their plates and ate in silence, but she was not going to be dissuaded. The women from her tennis club had all been to Southport.

Mary felt smug as they waited for the train the following weekend: she'd made all the arrangements for their holiday and secured a house just a short walk from the beach for two guineas a week.

At Bethania Junction, the guard came through the carriages announcing that there were precisely seventeen minutes left to get a pie and a cup of tea. Jackie, Madge and Hazel spent the seventeen minutes watching the engine crew drop the ash and take on water and coal for the rest of the trip. The pie was glutenous, the tea luke-warm.

At Southport, the family transferred to a bus that dropped them, with their luggage, on the side of the road. They waded through deep, loose sand, struggling with heavy suitcases, to reach their holiday cottage.

Mary opened the kitchen cupboard with its green and white glass door. There she found four chipped cups and three saucers. She sighed. Standing behind, Jack put his arms around her. 'Don't worry love, Jackie doesn't like drinking tea, and I can do without a saucer.'

The pure white Queensland sand stretched for miles in either direction. Waves, not very big ones, rolled and frothed over each other as Mary spread a rug on the sand and sat under her extra wide hat.

'Aren't you coming in?' asked Jack.

'I don't like swimming.'

'Then why on earth did you want to come to the beach?'

Taking Madge and Hazel by the hand, Jack led his two daughters into the sea. Mary noticed that Madge, in her woollen bathers, was taking on the shape of a woman.

They were only in the water half an hour, but Madge emerged red as a beetroot from sunburn. Jack walked towards Mary with his head on the side.

'What's wrong with you?'

'I think I've got water in my ear.'

'It might do it some good.'

This was the ear that had been bayoneted, the ear that Mary syringed every week with salty water. Surely that was no different from bathing in the ocean? But that night, the pain in Jack's ear became unbearable, and he couldn't sleep. This wasn't the normal colourless discharge that stained his pillowcase at night. After a couple of days, it became milky and smelled foul.

For the next week Madge stayed out of the sun and Jack, his head wrapped in a thick cotton scarf, read on the front verandah. Jackie, who did not want to be at the beach, remained belligerent.

Hazel was the only one who enjoyed the holiday. Dark haired and olive skinned, she splashed in the shallow water and built imaginative sandcastles in the sand with Mary watching from beneath her hat.

At Bethania Junction on the trip home Mary said: 'I think we should go to the mountains next year'.

Jack looked at her, and threw his eyes upwards. They didn't have the pie and cuppa on offer.

❧

As the world began its economic slide in 1928, railway workers, fearing dismissal, flocked to the ARU despite attempts by the AWU to poach them. State Council decided there was a greater need to have organisers on the road than secretaries in the Trades Hall office, and so abolished the district offices, reclassifying the secretaries as organisers, and requiring sub-branches to attend to petty grievances and routine office work. This left the organisers free to sign up new members and represent existing ones at inquiries and appeals. The executive then issued each district organiser with a motorbike.

❧

Mary opened the front gate, and in rode Jack astride a flat-tank AJS with a metal badge, bearing the letters *A.R.U.*, standing erect on the front mudguard.

'Hop on,' he said, nodding to the seat behind him.

'Oh, I don't think so, Jack!'

'Why not?'

She hitched up her skirt and climbed on, gripping Jack's waist for dear life. He turned a slow circle in the side yard, and drove out the front gate.

'Lean with me,' he shouted over his shoulder as they came to the first corner. She did, and to her amazement, didn't fall off. Back in the yard, Madge refused to get on, but Hazel bounced up and down demanding to be allowed.

'No Jack, she's too little.'

'Nonsense. You're a big girl, aren't you Hazel?'

Hazel scrambled up behind her father and he ever so gently rode around and around the side yard. They were still enjoying the bike when Jackie arrived home from secondary school. He jumped on the back and said, 'Where are we going Dad?'

Jack took off down the road much faster than Mary thought he should.

Jack's home now become his base. His district committee asked for a telephone to be installed to enable state officials to reach him whenever necessary, and the committee debated the issue for a month, but ultimately decided against doing so. As he would be on the road more often than at home, the expenditure was not warranted.

~

On May Day in 1929, the Trades Hall unions boycotted what they considered a capitalists' procession. Then came the state election campaign. Most references linking McCormack to political corruption were muted, as the Premier made no secret of the fact that he would sue anyone who published libellous material. This did not stop George, who continued his attack through *The Advocate*:

> McCormack has 'dodged' the issue of the Mungana purchase, though it stinks in the nostrils of the Labour Movement.

George could not write in support of the scab-or-be-sacked McCormack Government, and therefore left union members to make up their own minds on voting.

Moore, Leader of the Opposition, promised much that the voters wanted to hear: he would re-open the Chillagoe smelters as a co-operative, run by the local miners; he would guarantee new jobs for the increasing army of unemployed; he would appoint a Royal Commissioner to inquire into the Chillagoe-Mungana affair - all the people of Queensland had to do was 'Give the Boy a Chance'.

Despite his union having disaffiliated with the Labor Party and the enmity that existed between them, Jack remained secretary of the Annerley Branch of the party and campaigned for the local candidate.

Come election day, the whole O'Leary family became involved. Jack left early for the voting booth, taking Madge and Jackie with him to hand out how-to-vote cards. Mary had arranged to supply sandwiches and flasks of tea (for a price) to the scrutineers. At twelve o'clock Hazel struggled up the road with a suitcase, and returned with the money.

Jack didn't arrive home till nearly midnight, less than sober. His electorate of Oxley had gone to the Tory, Nimmo, and McCormack's Government had been well and truly trounced. After fourteen years, the workers of Queensland finally said no to a Labor Government, preferring a government that owed nothing to the labour movement over a government that had turned its back on them.

Jack felt vindicated: the hatred and bitterness he and other members of his union had been exposed to in the past few years had not gone unnoticed by other unions. The Australian Railways Union, intent on over-throwing McCormack's Government, had mostly voted informally, and these protest votes had made a tangible difference to the outcome.

Still, electoral defeat was a bitter pill for George, Tim and Jack to swallow, knowing their fight would now be much harder having to deal with a conservative government. As it turned out, the Right was not the only faction they had to deal with. In the union's Central District office of Rockhampton, Walbank, who sat on State Council, submitted a long and vitriolic letter to *The*

Advocate, expressing anger at the lack of direction during the election campaign from the union executive. As editor, George's brief from State Council was to keep *The Advocate* free of libellous material and prevent disaffection and conflict. George judged the letter to be neither educative, nor propaganda for the good of the union and refused to publish it; a decision that was to ultimately end his reign as union president.

∾

The belch burnt all the way up to his throat. A painful belch. Bill McCormack replaced the stopper in the blue glass bottle and reached for the Stanbeck's powder, although he doubted its ability to shift the vice gripping his head. Forgan Smith's Scottish brogue exacerbated the ex-Premier's irritability.

'If you think you should resign, then I canna stop you, Mac.'

McCormack pressed his palm into his ribcage, but he knew his heart pain wouldn't ease either.

'I'm sick Bill. If I don't quit, this'll probably kill me. We've lost sixteen seats. Sixteen! It's unprecedented.'

He belched again as the bromo-seltzer began its work on his troubled intestines.

A week later, with his nerves shot, his guts aching and his heart skipping beats, McCormack handed the party leadership to Forgan Smith. Hoping he could now get on with life and put the whole bitter business behind him, he set sail for London to receive specialist treatment for his troubled heart.

∾

Jack packed his case, strapped it to the back of the AJS, and again headed north to organise for the union. This time, he had to cover his entire district and would be away for a month, well into September.

Money was short in the O'Leary household. Jackie, still at secondary school, wrote weekly columns for the sports page of *The Daily Standard* and contributed what money he could, but Madge, now thirteen and finished her schooling, had no ideas for her future. Mary decided Madge should look for work, but work was not to be found. Each day, mother and daughter went to the city enquiring at all the shops, always receiving the same reply: 'I'm sorry Miss, we've had to put workers off. We won't be employing anyone for quite a while.'

After a modest lunch at a cafeteria, they would catch the bus back home.

Madge was much more present in Mary's life than Jack was. In Mary's view, a woman doesn't belong in the world of railway unions, not when her husband is away, no matter how much she takes their welfare to heart, and so mother and daughter slipped into a companionship that excluded the rest of the world.

Jack had only been on this trip two weeks when they heard the bike pull into the front yard and Jack climb the front stairs, coughing. Mary took one look at him, felt his forehead, and sent him to bed while Madge walked up to Ipswich Road to fetch the doctor.

'Jack appears to have a dose of influenza. You're good at looking after him Mrs O'Leary so just do the usual. Plenty of hot lemon drinks and your hearty Scottish broth. I'll call tomorrow after surgery and check on him.'

When Doctor Holmes left, Mary went to the bedroom.

'I've gotta get back and finish my rounds,' said Jack.

'You're delirious, Jack. Otherwise you wouldn't suggest such a thing.'

He'd completed his tour north of Brisbane and had been heading for the South Coast when he fell ill, and had steered for home instead.

'You can go back when you're better. I'll let George know you're home.'

George visited two nights later.

'I must say, you don't look too well.' But the racking cough drowned his words.

Outside the bedroom George said, 'Don't let him come back to work until he's fully recovered, Mary. Those damn bikes don't offer any protection from the wind or rain. I fear it was a mistake not holding out for motor cars.'

After two weeks, Jack felt well enough to join the family for the evening meal. He bathed and dressed for dinner. Mary made a special effort: roast mutton, lots of vegetables, even a rice pudding. But it all remained uneaten.

The effort Jack had made to join the dinner table brought on a fresh fit of coughing. He held his handkerchief to his mouth, and as he coughed into it, Jackie, Madge, Hazel and Mary watched in horror as a small pink patch appeared in the centre. Jackie bolted for the door and ran to fetch Doctor Holmes. As Mary gently laid him back in bed, the look of fear in his eyes matched her own.

Later, in the kitchen, Doctor Holmes said the words Mary did not wish to hear: 'I'll arrange for tests, but I think we have to conclude Jack has tuberculosis'.

Mary closed her eyes. The room spun.

'Has he always had this weakness in the chest?' asked the doctor.

'Only since the war. Before that, he was always healthy.'

'Did anything happen during the war that could have caused this? Was he gassed?'

'Not so far as I know. If he was, he never mentioned it.' Then she remembered. 'His ship was torpedoed, and he spent some time in icy water.'

'That would have done it. Many returned soldiers who suffered exposure now have TB. I suspect his lungs were damaged during the episode, and that's made him vulnerable.'

'But surely that wouldn't have caused TB?'

'No, not directly. But he would have been a sitting target for the bacterium to take hold.'

Doctor Holmes collected his coat and hat: 'I'll send the sample of his sputum off for testing tomorrow'.

When the doctor left, Mary went to the darkened bedroom and sat on the side of the bed. She could feel the heat radiating from Jack, his clothes saturated with sweat. She thought he was asleep, but he rolled onto his back.

Softly, he said 'I heard everything Doctor Holmes said. It looks bad, love.'

Mary cried. He pulled her gently onto his chest and stroked her hair and she could hear his lungs gurgling.

The tests confirmed he had TB.

Chapter 12 - Sedition (1929-1930)

The high walls of the Supreme Court dwarfed Frederick Reid as he faced the examiner for the Public Curator. He cared little that McGill's questions were sidestepping the central issue: that of a declaration of bankruptcy against himself and Goddard. They had worked as a team before and would do so again once they rid themselves of the unsuccessful hotel in Cairns. It was just a matter of time. Now he looked directly into the piercing eyes as the barrister asked in a resonant voice: 'Mr. Reid, could you please tell the court who were some of the most prominent shareholders in Mungana Mines when you held the lease?'

'McCormack was the most prominent.'

'Did he back you and finance you?'

'No. I did not want any.'

'Did he not put in anything?'

'He put in about £100.'

The judge interrupted the examination: 'Mr. Reid, what did you agree to give him for that interest?'

'I agreed to give him half the profits I received.'

The examiner for the Public Curator clarified: 'Half the profits?'

'Yes.'

Again the judge interjected: 'Under your agreement with Mr McCormack did you give him £5,000 of shares?'

'Yes.'

'This, Your Honour,' said the examiner, 'is considerably more than 388 shares, is it not?'

The next day, Queensland Parliament erupted. Bill Kelso who, three years before had checked the companies' register and found McCormack had shares in Mungana, addressed the House.

'Mr Speaker, I say that Mungana is only a trifle compared to the concessions given by McCormack, Theodore and Jones; men who ought to have *protected* the public purse of Queensland.'

'Hear, hear!'

'I allege that certain former cabinet ministers of years past received parcels of Mount Isa shares upon safe passage of the Duchess to Mount Isa Railway Bill in 1925. These men, Mr Speaker, utilised public funds and prostituted the high offices which they held in this State!'

Randolph Bedford - member for Warrego and friend of Theodore and Wren - who feared his own name might be sullied in the blame game, rose to defend his colleagues.

'Mr Speaker, the shares to the three gentlemen mentioned were merely gestures of *friendship*. The member for Nundah is attempting to blacken the name of Mr Theodore and Mr McCormack to create public enthusiasm for an inquiry into Chillagoe and Mungana. And I suggest further, Mr Speaker, that this is a political stunt, as it is no coincidence that Mr Theodore, as deputy leader of the federal Labor Party, will soon be facing the people of Australia at election.'

Moore, the Premier of Queensland, rose to his feet and delivered a decision over which he had pondered long and hard: 'Mr Speaker, Ministers of the Crown and other members of Parliament must be above suspicion. It is therefore my intention to call a Royal Commission into the conduct at Chillagoe Smelters and Mungana Mines to ascertain who is guilty and whether we can prosecute.'

The Speaker could not contain the ensuing uproar.

&

It took a few weeks, but Jack's coughing did subside and his appetite returned along with the colour to his cheeks. He strapped his case back onto the bike and continued organising, gang-to-gang.

He was 'riding the lengths' when prices plummeted on the New York Stock Exchange on that infamous Tuesday in October. The next day he rode towards Ipswich and headlong into a sandstorm. At first, he took the brown cloud over the paddocks for a rainstorm, but as it rolled closer grains of sand stung his bare face and hands. He squinted as the barrage increased, and slowed to a crawl. Then the sand cloud covered him and his bike. A pain shot through his left eye and he could see nothing. He dropped his bike and hunkered down behind it, with grit trapped between eyeball and eyelid, for half an hour. When the terrible wind had passed it left a thick coating of sand on everything and an unearthly still silence. Jack swept the sand from his bike and hauled it back to the road, willing someone to come. Through a blurry veil across his eyes all he could see in either direction was a long strip that had once been a ribbon of bitumen - now the same sand colour as the fields flanking it.

Mounting his bike, he crawled the thirty miles into Ipswich, looking for the first sign of a farmhouse, now hoping no one else would be stupid enough to be on the road. When he finally saw the outline of a building through his weeping eyes, he puttered into the yard, dodging three dogs barking at his ankles. A woman stood on the verandah, fists on hips, as he kicked the bike onto its stand. He spoke to her with eyes red and running.

'Could you please help me, I got caught in the storm and I can't see.'

He arrived at the Ipswich Hospital in the front of the farm truck with his bike on the tray.

Mary and Madge had been in the city doing the usual rounds asking for employment, and arrived home to find Jack in the kitchen with a patch over his right eye. There was no sign of the bike.

'I hit a sandstorm west of Ipswich, and I've been virtually blind for the past week.'

'How did you get home?' Mary asked.

'By train. They put the bike in the goods carriage - someone'll bring it home tonight. George met me at the station and drove me home.'

'Have you seen a doctor?'

'Yes. He put some drops in my eyes that made them sting. He removed most of the grains but there's still three in my right eye. One's lodged in the pupil, and he doesn't like the chances of removing it.'

The next day, George drove Jack to a specialist, but all he could do was supply a pair of spectacles with side patches to block the glare and lenses of finely punched metal.

≈

After the crash of the world's stock markets, the papers were full of doom. Because Jack's eyes were still troubling him, it fell to Mary to read the papers aloud each evening, commencing with *The Daily Standard*, then progressing to other papers in turn. One evening, Mary read with disbelief from *The Advocate*: 'One miner killed and nine injured in mine clashes. Police fire on massed pickets at Rothbury Mine. Nine constables hurt in serious rioting. Reinforcements rushed from Sydney.'

She looked up from the paper, feeling vulnerable. 'Oh God!' She continued:

> The New South Wales Government moved scabs into the small mine at Rothbury. It is estimated there were six thousand picketing the mine. The picketers' aim was to threaten the scabs who had taken their jobs, but as they crossed the fence at first light, the police opened fire.
>
> In their defence, the police claimed to have fired above their heads. They must be bad shots! Many miners were wounded in the subsequent baton charge. A seventy-year-old was batoned to his knees.
>
> Norman Brown, twenty-eight, wasn't even on the line at the time he was shot in the stomach, he had been sitting talking to a girlfriend. He died on the way to hospital.

They sat in silence when she finished the article.

'No-one'll be called to answer for it, any more than they were called to answer for the shooting of Andy Hynes at South Johnstone,' said Jack.

'Is this madness ever going to end?' Mary asked.

'Not until we get a government that genuinely cares about its workers. Until then, the madness will continue.'

And continue it did.

By November 1929 the Australian Railways Union was sucked into the vortex of belt-tightening restrictions that consumed the world. To add to the union's woes, the Moore State Government decided to stop giving preference to unionists in the railway service in Queensland.

A sense of desperation infiltrated the union as each member felt his working security threatened. They argued about how the union ought to be run and sent letters to *The Advocate*. The Central Executive in Brisbane wanted to hang on to the staff at all costs; they knew their members responded well to regular visits from their organisers, but not everyone was convinced.

❧

Cursing Frank Ryan, and weary at heart, Gwen eased her back on the leather train seat, bone-tired from thirty hours jolting and swaying. All she'd eaten were greasy pies swilled down with weak refreshment-room tea, most of which she had lost over the wrought-iron rail at the end of her carriage.

Tree-clad mountains slid by monotonously, the clacketty-clack rose in pitch as the train crossed a bridge, then resumed its constant rhythm. She dozed on and off. Waking with a crick in her neck, she watched the houses pass in quick succession as they neared South Brisbane station.

The last time she had arrived in Brisbane, she had been single and been met by her lover. Now she was married, pregnant, and alone. Again she cursed her husband. Struggling with her cardboard case, she boarded a tram and headed for New Farm, wondering if she should have written her mother before arriving, but she had no words adequate to describe the awfulness of the past two years.

All the windows were closed and the curtains drawn, and at first Gwen thought Gladys was not at home. She knocked loudly and from the rear of the house came the rustling of papers and measured footsteps. The door opened an inch and her mother's eyes appeared at the crack.

'What you want?'

'It's me, Mum.'

The door opened enough for Gladys's head to poke through.

'God, girl. You look awful!'

She opened the door wide and stood aside for Gwen to enter.

'You on your own, then?'

Gwen cried three months of pent-up tears onto the soft bosom of her mother.

Sitting at the table, face-to-face, neither Gwen nor Gladys knew what to say next. Two years had passed since Gwen left for Sydney, and neither had written.

'Aunt Mildred's dead, Mum.'

'Yeah, I heard.'

Gwen wondered how her mother would have heard of the death of her father's sister, but she didn't ask.

'I also heard you married that no-hoper.'

'He's my husband, Mum. He's not a no-hoper, just gets caught.'

'Is that why you're here now. Did he get caught?'

Gladys waited for Gwen's fresh bout of tears to settle.

'He got five years this time, Mum. He set fire to a house he'd robbed. What am I gunna do?'

'You're pregnant, aren't you?'

Gwen nodded.

'It's not me first one. I've lost two. I was five months with 'em both. I'm scared, Mum.'

'You can stay here, girl. I wouldn't put you out.'

Gwen's 'thanks' was lost in muffled sobs.

❧

One very hot morning, with Christmas decorations still adorning the city shop windows and thunderclouds building behind One Tree Hill in the west, the O'Leary family went to the Domain to hear the Sunday spruikers - only this was no ordinary day. The Moore Government was threatening to pass the Industrial Conciliation and Arbitration Act Amendment Bill, designed to allow police to gaol strikers, and Fred Paterson, who two years before had left his pig farm and moved to Brisbane to study law, was to speak against the proposed bill.

From his soapbox, he pulled no punches:

If the workers shed a little blood in their own interests, as they did for the capitalists in the war, they would be emancipated. They should take the law into their own hands. Although I hope I will not have to shed any of my blood, if necessity arises, I am willing to do so in conjunction with the workers as a whole. But if I do so the workers would have to be thoroughly organised to have a successful issue. There was no harm in the spilling of blood in the late war in the capitalists' interests, so why could it not be spilt in the workers' interests, who could not be much worse off than they are now?

'Good on you, Fred.' Jack could not contain himself.

At the conclusion of his speech, Fred left the soapbox and joined Jack.

'Fine speech, Fred.'

'Thanks, but I doubt our two police friends thought so.'

He nodded towards the plain-clothes policemen, pen and notebook in hand, comparing notes. 'I expect there'll be trouble.'

Just over two weeks later, George's phone rang as he was putting the final touches to the month's *Advocate*. It was Fred Paterson.

'Sorry to bother you, George. At the moment I'm a guest of His Majesty in the Watch House. I need someone to stand surety before they grant bail. How are you fixed?'

'Shit, Fred. What happened?'

'I've been arrested for sedition. They didn't like my speech at the Domain a couple of weeks ago.'

'I'll be right there.'

Of course, Fred's was to be a political trial: if found guilty of sedition, he would not be able to become a barrister. Fred could not afford to engage a solicitor and so, with his final bar examination just weeks away, he took time out from his studies to prepare his own defence. Wisely, as it turned out.

With the deepening depression, many who had once been militant unionists (often members of the Communist Party) needed somewhere to direct their anger and so, worldwide, the One Big Union for the Unemployed was formed. These people had many years' experience in organising, and the union became a force to be reckoned with. Other unionists, protective of their own jobs, feared the OBU's growing influence and shunned them - all except the Australian Railways Union. Tim Moroney attended most of their meetings, speaking when he had something to say, supporting them in their many campaigns.

When Fred Paterson was arrested, thousands of angry men and women gathered outside the watch-house, shouting at the walls, calling for Fred's release. Police arrived wielding batons, so the mob reassembled the following day in the meeting room of Trades Hall.

A resolution was put, and carried:

> That the OBU of Unemployed strongly objects to the attitude of the Moore Government in suppressing the right of free speech, and in the subsequent arrest of FW Paterson for placing the doctrines of the working class before the workers in the Domain on January 12.

When Fred finally came to trial, Jack and Mary squeezed into the courtroom and heard the two policemen give evidence who, in their stupidity, gave the same report, word for word. Fred had little trouble convincing the jury their evidence was fabricated. He was found not guilty.

'There's a modicum of justice in the world, then,' Mary said.

'Only because the jury was made up of workers!' replied Jack.

❦

Bill McCormack pulled his dressing gown across his stomach and tied the silk cord, welcoming the coolness of the verandah boards on the soles of his bare feet. Sleep evaded him, but this was nothing new. A waning moon hung overhead, not offering much light to the quiet streets of Annerley. The front door opened, and his sister's shadow split the hallway light spilling onto the verandah.

'Bill. You'll never get to sleep wandering about out here.'

Four years older than her brother and the oldest of the McCormack siblings, Flora always spoke with authority.

'Do you have pain? I thought you'd be your old self again after your spell in London.'

'No. No pain.'

'Then why are you up at this ungodly hour?'

'I'm going to resign, Flora.'

Even in the faint light on the verandah, he saw the colour drain from her face. She sank to a chair and the canvas creaked all the louder for the stillness of the night.

'You can't, Bill. Being in Parliament means everything to you!'

'I have to, Flora. Don't worry about the money, I'm pretty comfortably off with my investments. I'll be able to support us.'

'Heavens! It's not the money. Surely you have pride?'

'Ah, pride. I think I might have left it in London with the heart surgeon. I can't continue, it'll kill me eventually. There's something else: the Terms of Reference have been set for the Royal Commission. It looks like they're going to dig deep, Flora.'

'Do you have to appear?'

'If they call me, I'll plead ill-health.'

He turned his back to his sister and leant on the rail: 'You go to bed Flora, I'll stay out here awhile'.

Flora lightly kissed the stubble on his craggy cheek, and thought she could smell fear.

On 21 February, Bill McCormack resigned his seat in Parliament and sank into the squatter's chair on his front verandah to be fussed over by his spinster sisters.

In May 1930, Hazel came home from school to find Mary at the kitchen table crying, a letter in her hand. She sat in the chair opposite, rested her chin on the table, and asked: 'What's wrong, Mummy?'

Mary had never met Margaret O'Leary, but she loved her son. For sixteen years the two women had corresponded, and now Jack's mother was dead.

When Jack arrived home from work that evening, Mary read to him the letter from his brother Ted. They sat well into the night, in silence, in the dark, mourning from the far side of the world.

~

George fought bitterly against suggestions to dispense with the services of organisers. Surely their job was even more important with dwindling numbers in the workforce and hence the union? In Rockhampton Walbank, still smarting over George's decision against publishing any of his propaganda in *The Advocate*, convinced the members of his District Committee that their organiser, Gordon Crane, would be the first to lose his job and the best thing for the union would be to get rid of their president. The rest was easy.

~

The first hint of autumn entered the arched windows of meeting room 45, stirring a light coating of dust on the windowsill. Conspiratorial murmurs filled the room. Six men huddled around a short man with horn-rimmed spectacles, their reflections distorted in the thick pebbles. Walbank pushed the frame back up his hooked nose with his index finger, his eyes magnified through the glass.

From the committee table at the far end of the room came the clink of glass on glass as Miss Mulvihill filled thirteen glasses from a water jug. The autumn breeze picked up, ruffling the sheets of the open minute book in the centre of the table. She set the jug on the table and, crossing to the sash window, pulled it almost closed.

No detail of the whispers could be heard beyond the immediate circle of the seven men, but it was obvious from the body language that Walbank had important information to share. Much shorter than the others before him, he stretched his neck endeavouring to see eye to eye.

The group's attention was focussed on a man who had, until now, remained on the edge. His suit was of a lesser quality than the other six, and threads protruded from the edge of his shirt collar. He shifted uneasily on his scuffed shoes.

This man, Guilfoyle, didn't really belong with this group, all from the Central District, who'd cornered him as soon as he'd entered the meeting room. Despite attending State Council of the union to represent the South-western District, all he wanted was to get his expenses paid. He could do with the money right now. His position of loco-running rep. did not cover what he lost each Saturday at the track.

Walbank's thick lenses misted and he wished the young woman had not closed the window. In hushed tones, he addressed Guilfoyle: 'We've got the numbers to have your expenses paid. If you back us, we'll back you.'

'That'd be good,' replied Guilfoyle. 'They've been refusing to pay me the three quid for six months; reckoned I didn't have approval to travel to Toowoomba to conduct the appeal.'

'Yeah, well, that's ancient history now,' said Walbank. 'We'll move for you to get paid, and you can vote with us for the rest of Council.'

'What you got in mind?' asked Guilfoyle.

'We're going to get rid of Rymer.'

'Get rid of Rymer! Jesus!' Guilfoyle stepped away from the circle, the shock on his face was visible to all in the room.

'Shh! Keep it under your hat for now,' said Walbank. 'We'll make our move later in the session.'

⫷

George tapped the water jug with his pen, calling the session to order. The seven conspirators took their places around the table beside George, Tim and four others who were unaware of the impending dropping of a bombshell.

The minutes of the previous meeting were read and adopted, then correspondence, inwards and outwards, dealt with. Federal matters were addressed. Tim reported that, immediately the Moore Government's Arbitration Act had been proclaimed, the Commissioner for Railways had challenged various sections of the Railway Award. The Council talked of how a female gatekeeper had replaced two male officers and was expected to carry out most of the work formerly done by them, at about a quarter the rate of pay previously paid to the men.

Then Walbank moved: 'That the amount as claimed by Comrade Guilfoyle be passed for payment'.

The animated debate continued for half an hour, but when the vote was taken, it succeeded seven to six.

Guilfoyle looked around the table catching Walbank's eye, and the delegate from Central District knew Rymer's hours were numbered. Walbank addressed Council saying that, in his opinion, it was time Council addressed the financial state of the union. Reorganisation was well and truly due. He proposed the position of paid state president be dispensed with and an honorary state president be appointed. He regretted that this would leave *The Advocate* without an editor, but he was sure this role could be competently filled by the state secretary. Guilfoyle, who could not look his president in the face, made much of studying the notes before him.

When Walbank finished his speech, he proposed: 'That the state president and editor, George Rymer, be notified that the agreement between himself and this organisation will be terminated as from 30 June next; that his services will not be required from the rising of Council; that he be paid for any leave due to him, also three months pay in lieu of notice'.

George, from the chair, broke the stunned silence: 'Does any man wish to speak against this motion?'

'Bloody oath!' said McLary, the executive member from Toowoomba who, in 1925, had opposed the signing of the anti-Communist pledge. 'It is clear that Comrade Walbank's motion for the abolition of the office of full-time state president is the culmination of a recently developed and keenly fought vendetta between the councillors from the Central District and Comrade Rymer. I speak for my committee when I say that if the motives which at present appear to be at the bottom of this movement are as I suspect, then this is one of the greatest acts of vengeance that, perhaps, this union has been subjected to. And that is saying something. I cannot believe that this fight, which began with the censoring of Walbank's letter by the editor of *The Advocate*, is to end in the tragedy of the abolition of an important office of the organisation.

'We, as a union, have considered many economy measures but never before has the union considered the abolition of the state presidency. I repeat: to lose our president would be a tragedy. It would appear, from where I stand, that a pact has today been made between the Central delegates and Comrade Guilfoyle.'

But the vote was put, and carried seven to five. George did not feel he could take part in the count.

Before Council rose three days later, the structure of the Queensland Branch of the Australian Railways Union was changed beyond recognition. As well as George's position, the district organiser positions were abolished and Jack was to receive three months notice. The whole state was to be divided into just two districts, with Jack appointed acting district secretary until permanent appointments could be made by Council.

Jack could accept the union's decision to eliminate his position - he knew these were difficult times for the union financially - but he could not accept what happened to his friend George, so he accompanied him to the pub where they proceeded to get well and truly drunk.

Madge woke Mary around seven o'clock the following morning.

'Mum. Are you awake?'

Mary pulled herself out of her dreams and looked at the clock. Then she noticed Jack's side of the bed hadn't been slept in. She sat up with a start.

'Dad's outside. I think he's been drinking.' Madge's top lip curled towards her nose in disgust. Mary pulled on her dressing gown, tying the cord as she opened the French doors. The front gate and verandah gate were wide open, and stretched out on the squatter's chair, one leg over each of the wooden arms, hat pulled over his face, was her Jack - snoring as if to awaken the dead.

'Leave him to me,' she told Madge, who was only too happy to do so. Mary shook him. He snorted and rolled over, folding his arms. She shook him again. He impatiently waved his arms at the menace.

'Jack O'Leary!' Mary removed the hat from his face, and he screwed his eyes against the glare.

'Inside! Now!' she ordered and stormed off to the kitchen, listening for signs that he was following. Peering through the door of the kitchen, Jack came face to face with an angry wife, sitting with arms crossed, waiting.

He tripped over fresh air as he headed for the stove.

'You want a cuppa? - Dear?' An afterthought.

'What I want is an explanation!'

He pulled the kettle forward to boil, then sat down with a heavy sigh.

'Oh dear! What time's it?'

'Seven o'clock. What time did you get in last night?'

'Gee. I've no idea - but it doesn't feel like I've had much sleep.'

'Where were you?'

'Ah. Not sure. Me'n George had a few.'

'That's patently obvious.'

'Aw, Mary. Don't go on. I feel terrible.'

'Good!' She left the room to change out of her nightie. Dressed in night attire, she felt she did not have the advantage over an adversary in a suit, no matter how dishevelled. When she returned to the kitchen, Jack was slumped on the table, snoring again.

'What's the use!' She left him to it.

Jack did not resurface until mid-afternoon. Mary had taken to the front garden to do some pruning when she heard him drawing a bath. He appeared, freshly shaven, neatly dressed and bearing a rose he'd picked from the garden. She pretended not to see him.

He passed the rose beneath her nose. It tickled. She sneezed.

'Bless you.' A few moments' silence. 'I love you.'

Mary sat back on her heels, fighting tears.

'Just a slip Mary. It won't happen again.'

'Won't it?' She knew her husband too well to believe that one. He held out his hands and helped her to her feet.

&

Chapter 13 - The biter bitten (1930)

A crispness to the morning announced that autumn had arrived in Brisbane as the sun's rays slanted through an open window, glinting off a pair of gold cufflinks on immaculate white cuffs. In the absent-mindedness brought about by habit, James Campbell pinched one cuff and pulled it over his wrist, then the other, aware of the hum of mid-week bustle of people going about their business beyond the open window. He stepped into the path of the sun and turned, feeling its warmth on his back, to scan the black print on the document in the centre of the oak desk:

> To The Honourable JAMES LANG CAMPBELL, lately one of the Justices of Our Supreme Court of New South Wales.
>
> Greeting:
>
> Whereas it is expedient in the public interest that full and careful inquiry should be made into ...

Not for the first time, the retired judge wondered how his conclusions would affect the people of Australia at such a time as this. He had bitterly resented being forced to retire from the bench at seventy-two, despite attempting to falsify his age. That his mind was as sharp as a sixty-year-old's had not escaped the notice of Premier Moore, nor had the fact that he had been a bank officer and also knew the mining industry intimately: the very man to head an inquiry into politicians and management at Chillagoe.

Again, he tugged at his cuffs, then gathered the papers into the crook of his right arm and entered the dim, timber-lined room of the Land Court on the third floor of Brisbane's Executive Building to commence the inquiry.

He had expected members of the press to be present, but was taken aback at the sight of a packed courtroom. People lined the side walls. He sat at his bench and those who had arrived early enough sat on the edge of their seats, waiting for his words.

I have been directed by His Excellency the Governor, for and on behalf of George the Fifth, by the Grace of God, of Great Britain, Ireland, and the British Dominions beyond the seas, King, Defender of the Faith, Emperor of India, to give full and careful inquiry into the following: The circumstances surrounding and leading up to the appointment of Peter Louis Goddard as Chillagoe Mines Manager ...

Justice Campbell read, in detail, each of the eight terms of reference before him. As he reached the final point, members of the press gallery leaned forward, as one, and carefully noted:

'... and that it should be determined and reported as hereinafter required whether and if so in what respect and to what degree any Minister of the Crown or any person having any duty to the Government of Queensland was guilty of any conduct in relation to any of the abovementioned matters...'

There was little doubt that this Royal Commission was aimed at Theodore and McCormack. Justice Campbell then proceeded to call the first of 43 witnesses who would give evidence over the next two months. But despite being ordered to appear before the inquiry, neither McCormack nor Theodore attended. To his solicitor, Macrossan, McCormack explained that he had been advised by the federal Labor Party leader, Doc Evatt, not to attend as his holding shares in a company which sold a property to the Crown could be construed as an act of conspiracy; and besides, he was under such strain he was likely to end up in hospital.

Theodore, now Federal Treasurer and putting the finishing touches to the 1930 budget, scorned the hearing by Campbell whom he considered merely a pensioner enlivening his retirement. And he could no longer assure Mac not to worry since Reid had spilled the beans, telling the Commissioner that McCormack held thousands of shares in Mungana, not the 388 he'd earlier claimed. McGill, assisting the Commissioner, did not let this pass unnoticed:

> McCormack has deliberately misled Parliament and lied publicly to the extent of his interests which exceeded 388 shares by many thousands. Whether McCormack divided his profits with anybody else, we do not know, but we do know that he stated in Parliament that there were others in the syndicate. I therefore call for copies of his bank account in order to trace what became of the money that was paid to him.

McCormack and Theodore both knew what the Commissioner would find when Mac's banking details were tabled. Justice Campbell had played his trump card. He gave his report much thought before penning his response to the eighth term of reference, but felt he had no option but to write:

> It is a painful thing to have to say of men who have occupied high and responsible positions in the State that they have betrayed, for personal gain, the trust reposed in them and have acted corruptly and dishonourably. Yet that is the invidious duty I feel is imposed upon me by the view I take of the evidence put before me on this part of the inquiry. I find it impossible to avoid the conclusion that Messrs. Theodore, McCormack, Reid, and Goddard have been collectively and severally guilty of a dishonest exploitation of the State in the sale to the State of the Mungana Mines for £40,000.

> When it was established on evidence that Mr. Theodore received, promptly and regularly from time to time, one-half of Mr. McCormack's share of the fruits of the Mungana transaction, the whole of the antecedent facts acquire a new significance.

He signed his report and submitted it to Cabinet on 4 July 1930, all too aware he was signing the political death warrant of Ted Theodore, tipped to be the next Prime Minister. At the completion of his report, he presented 25 questions that he felt should be answered before a court of law. But Jack did not celebrate. He knew these two men carried enough influence to secure their own acquittal in any court of law.

❧

Before Jack's three-months' notice with the union had expired, he was offered the position of secretary for the newly-formed Southern Division, but with his health failing, he could not justify taking on a position he knew he could not fulfil. He was now off work for three weeks out of four. The time had come for him to leave the executive ranks of his union.

Since 1926, the O'Leary household got by on Jack's weekly income of £8 plus the £3 army pension he received as a result of his deafness. It came as something of a shock, therefore, to drop to just £3.

'You know Mary, there would be no harm in Madge taking a factory job. It might even do her some good.'

Mary stared at Jack in horror. 'No daughter of mine will work in a factory!'

'I don't see why you're so against the idea. It's not as if they're a lower class of human being, you know.'

'No! We'll be all right. Jackie will start work next year, and I'm sure Madge will find something. Soon.'

Even after all these years, Mary didn't totally share Jack's ideals of equality. He was truly an egalitarian man - there were no class barriers in his life - but Mary had been raised with the belief she was someone special, a belief she passed on to her children. However, she had also inherited from her mother the ability to feed a family on very little money.

There were parts of a sheep some people wouldn't eat, but she would, conjuring up sheep's head soup, sheep's feet stew, sheep's brain rissoles. Jack grew vegetables in the back yard, and the rabbit seller frequently knocked at the door. When the family didn't have enough money to pay for his rabbits, he gladly accepted vegetables in payment. They also kept chooks in a tumble-down pen under the mango tree. As a result their diet was varied and nutritious.

More frequently now, Jack's coughing produced blood-streaked mucous. Mary tore up old sheets for him to use as handkerchiefs and boiled them after use. The household settled into the routine of pouring boiling water over Jack's dishes and washing them separately from the rest of the family. Jack never mentioned that he felt like an outcast.

At the end of 1930 they visited the guesthouse in Mapleton again. Jackie, in his final year at secondary school, preferred to remain at home. Mary worried over this, but Jack said: 'He's sixteen, Mary. At his age I was at sea.'

At Mapleton, the owners of Strongarra were only too aware of the state of the world, and a week's board had only risen by 5/- in the four years since the O'Leary's last visit.

They read, played tennis, rode to Nambour on the cane train and walked through the peaceful forest. On New Year's Eve they danced in the village hall, but this year Mary could not kiss her husband at midnight. Curse this disease!

No sooner had Jackie finished school than he started as a reader at *The Daily Standard*. Despite the anti-ARU stance this paper had taken during the Hayes dispute, Jack was proud that his son worked for a labour newspaper. However, there was still no employment for Madge, and Mary did not push her. More and more she depended on her daughter's companionship.

Jack's union life was over but his political life wasn't. He remained secretary of the Annerley Branch of the Labor Party and filled his nights with reading, but the long hours of the day bored and frustrated him.

❧

- PART FOUR -

O God! That bread should be so dear,
And flesh and blood so cheap.

Thomas Hood (Punch, 1843)

Chapter 14 - Bailiffs and Batons (1931)

With the first twittering of the wrens, Tom Rickard crept from his hut deep within Toohey Forest. He had long grown used to his camp bed - hessian sacks pulled taut over a wooden frame - but last night he hadn't slept well, due as much to the clammy air as anticipation of the day ahead. He put a match to a bundle of sticks in the fire pit and hung a blackened billy on a hook suspended above it. As the water bubbled, nine other men left their own shelters and joined him by the fire.

When they had all filled their mugs from the billy, Tom tipped the dregs onto the fire. The liquid hissed as it doused the flames.

The ten men left camp and followed a path across a carpet of rust-coloured casuarina needles that muffled their tread. Casuarinas gave way to eucalypts, and the men formed into single file, gripping thin trunks to steady themselves as they slithered down the steep bank to Mimosa Creek. Pebbles rolled beneath the well-worn soles of their shoes. With the spring dryness of the past few months, the creek had become no more than a string of waterholes between tallowwood and scribbly gum.

A flock of small birds appeared in the canopy then disappeared as quickly, leaving the air thick with the scent of disturbed blossom. Reaching the bottom of the gully, the men turned west and followed the creek bed for a mile through thick stands of mat rush.

The path left the creek and rose sharply, winding around large Moorooka rocks covered with lichen and drooping fronds of shield ferns. Between the rocks, grass trees stood like statues: on one leg, each clothed in a skirt of grey-green strands with flower spikes rising where a head should have been. Honeyeaters buried their long slender beaks deep into the minute blossoms.

After a mile, as the gully narrowed and rose steadily towards Toohey Mountain, the men swung right onto a dirt road made by old man Toohey in the previous century - in the days when he called this land his own and turned his cattle out to graze amongst the trees.

Reaching the forest's edge, they crossed Mayfield Road and continued along Tooheys Road to a side street where six identical cottages stood, side by side. Tom tapped on the front window of the first house. The sun, clearing the horizon, glinted off the window as a woman lifted the corner of a curtain and peered out. She smiled recognition and withdrew a heavy bolt from the front door.

'Hello Lizzie. Word is, you'll be needing a hand today.'

The other men nodded 'G'day' to the young woman and filed into the hallway. Tom looked away from Lizzie's trembling hands as she pulled the bolt to.

'I'd offer you all a cuppa, but ...'

'No need, Lizzie love. We've all had something. You just take the kids next door and leave the rest to us.'

Lizzie Armitage, thirty years of age and rake thin, went to the bedroom and gently roused her three sleeping children from the double bed they shared. She lifted the youngest onto her hip and held out her hand for the three-year-old. Her big girl, now five, rubbed the sleep from her eyes and padded after her mother and two brothers.

Tom had known Lizzie's family for ten years; had worked at the Gabba Goods Yards with Cec until they were laid off in '29. It wasn't so bad for Tom. Without a wife or kids, he was able to move into the unemployed camp in Toohey Forest and eke out a living on 13/6 a week. But Cec had Lizzie and the kids to think of, so he went *on the wallaby* - after extracting a promise from Tom to look out for Lizzie - looking for work, periodically sending home money to keep his family housed and fed until things improved. The last Tom heard, Cec was out at Longreach, rouseabout at the shearing sheds. Despite Lizzie's home being a simple four-roomed cottage, she could no longer keep up the rent payments. The wood stove in the corner of the kitchen was cold, and the shelves contained just a bag of flour, a tin of tea and a few spuds beginning to sprout. The pine table in the centre of the kitchen, like the floorboards and the kids, was scrubbed clean.

'Keep back from the windows,' instructed Tom.

The men sat on the floor, backs to the wall. One patted his shirt pocket, feeling for his tobacco pouch, then remembered - no smoking. It would be a long wait.

An hour passed before they heard the chug of a motor vehicle pulling up outside. Tom, pressing flat against the wall, looked through a gap between the curtain and architrave. A tall man in gaberdine trousers and shirt, with the sleeves rolled past his elbows, climbed down from the flat-bed truck - 'That'd be the bailiff', thought Tom - and a portly man, in suit and Trilby, (the agent) stepped from the passenger's side door. As Tom watched, a police car pulled in behind the truck and a constable joined the other two men, tapping a baton on his left palm, testing its strength, signalling his readiness to use it.

'Action time, boys!' whispered Tom.

The ten men moved into the hallway. The police baton hit the front door with such force it splintered the wood.

'Easy on, constable, I don't want the door busted,' said the agent.

Tom waited until the third knock (get them good and mad) before opening the door. Surprised by the sight of 10 men when he had expected a worried woman, the constable brought his baton down with the same energy that he had used on the door, cracking Tom's skull, pulping his skin and matting his hair with blood. Tom vomited, reeled, and fell to his knees. In a daze, he saw the constable's five brass buttons wave, out of focus, above him; felt a wet warmth trickle down his cheek, then everything went black. The other nine men drew iron bars and rushed at the policeman, the bailiff and the agent, driving them back to their motor vehicles, jeering at the crunch of gears in their panic to get away.

Tom came to with Lizzie bandaging his head.

'Did we get them?'

'Shush, Tom. Stay still, you've been hurt bad.'

'Did we get them!'

'Yeah, they're gone for now.'

An off-white sheet of paper fluttered around thumbtacks on the power pole. The letters, blurred at the edges, had been typed by two fingers onto a stencil which was then laid on a flat-bed duplicator for ink to be rolled along by hand; but the message was clear:

Unemployed meeting here tonight at 7 o'clock.

Jack pulled his watch from his waistcoat pocket. Still over an hour to wait. He walked further along Ipswich Road to the Annerley pub to fill in time before the meeting. He had been unemployed for twelve months, although Mary did not see it that way. Her husband, she told her tennis-playing friends, had retired due to ill health. And there was no denying this was true. But Jack knew he was unemployed. And so he went along to the meetings of the Unemployed Workers Movement. Like many of the others who attended, he kept his pride: dressed in his suit; wore his hat with the crease in the crown kept sharp by a tap from the side of his hand.

Jack approached the bar and ordered a shandy - his way of staying off the grog - and saw Tom Rickard leaning on it. Years ago, at the Gabba Goods Yards, Jack, Tom and Cec had made a good team. When Jack left the Yards and moved to Trades hall, they had met now and then for a beer. Now, paid off like the rest of them, Tom did not consider himself unemployed as he put his skills to use organising for the Movement. He had arranged this evening's meeting. Tom lifted his glass in a wave, inviting Jack to join him.

'I hear Fred Paterson's talking tonight,' said Jack.

'Yeah, Fred always draws a crowd. He'll be giving us the low-down on what's happening in the Soviet Union,' replied Tom. The beer brought a flush to his chubby cheeks. He removed his hat and with a folded handkerchief, mopped his brow - a brow that extended high on his head and was fringed by sandy frizz.

'The bailiff visited Lizzie yesterday,' said Tom.

'Shit! Did he get anything?'

'No, we convinced him to leave. I'd say the agent's scared though, as he slipped a note in her letter box last night giving her another fortnight to come up with the rent.'

Tom took another gulp of beer. 'We'd better make damn sure she's safe,' he continued. 'Cec. would expect it of us. I'll be organising a squad tonight.'

Jack stretched his long sinewy neck and upended his glass, just as the publican called 'Time'.

The air inside the weatherboard hall tasted sour of sweat and cigarette smoke as men and women crushed through its doorway and lined the walls. Every position on every wooden form was filled with people eager to hear a solution. From the side of the hall near the doorway Jack could see familiar faces in the crowd, including many railway workers. Tom left Jack to find a seat and walked to the front of the hall to welcome the crowd and introduce Fred Paterson. The din lowered to a whisper, then complete silence.

'Good evening ladies and gentlemen, it's very encouraging to see so many here this evening to hear what the Communist Party of Australia has to offer in these troubled times. I won't waste words when pictures can tell the story.'

Tom turned out the lights and a square of light filled the screen behind Fred. For an hour, the crowd watched lantern-slides of life in the Soviet Union as Fred explained how the five-year plan was successfully tackling poverty by offering jobs, and providing the necessities of life: food, clothing, subsidised housing, education - and hope for a better future. He drew comparisons with Australia where the poor and dispossessed, adults and children alike, were victims of the crisis, and the government provided the most meagre relief. When the slide show had finished, he answered many questions and handed out leaflets.

Tom thanked Fred for an enlightening show, and everyone for their attention, then said: 'As you all know, many families live in fear of eviction. They have to live five families to a house sometimes - and the owners are threatening to kick them out because they can't meet the rent. We need to make sure the cops and bailiffs don't get anywhere near the front doors.'

'All it takes is manpower,' called one man, 'and there's no shortage of that here'.

'You'd think so.' replied Tom. 'A number of the picketers have ended up in Boggo Road, and that scares off many who'd normally get involved; but there's no reason to worry about being arrested. If you are, contact Fred.'

Fred smiled to himself: despite the efforts from powerful men in government, he had successfully passed his Bar exams at a time when almost one in three workers was unemployed, and he was finding no shortage of people to represent. He was rarely paid for his services, but kept secret his own straightened circumstances; no one knew he had borrowed the coat he wore for his first court appearance. Neither did he speak of his wife's infidelities that had led to his divorcing Lucy.

Tom continued: 'I want to tell you about Mrs Armitage, a woman living on her own with three kids. Her hubby was a decent worker on the railways, always paid his union dues and did a fair day's work, that was until the Moore Government paid him off two years back along with many other railway workers. Since then, he's been on the track looking for any work he can get. Yesterday, the agent tried to kick Mrs Armitage out of her home because she can't pay the rent. I know many of you in this room are in a similar situation, but in fourteen days he'll be back to try again, and this time, he won't muck around. Anyone who can help, please see me after tonight's meeting. These bastards need to be taught a lesson!'

Two hundred men remained after the meeting.

Sparks rose as Tom threw a log on the fire. Crimson flames licked its bark, eddied around a knot-hole, then engulfed the log, drawing it into the heart of the fire. His head still ached, but five days after the bashing, the wound was healing okay. To his left and his right sat the ten men of the Tarragindi anti-eviction committee. Tom had invited Jack to meet with them to organise their plan of attack to safeguard Lizzie Armitage. When Jack appeared from the surrounding bushes, he approached the men and sat on his haunches and rolled a cigarette.

'Good camp,' he said.

'Yeah, it's not bad,' replied Tom.

With thumb and forefinger, Jack pulled a box of matches from his shirt pocket and lit his cigarette. Tom hooked a spare crate with his boot and pulled it over for Jack, then handed him a mug of black tea. Jack shook his head: 'Thanks Tom, but best not share your mug: TB'. He thumped his chest. Tom nodded in understanding and introduced Jack.

'This's Jack O'Leary, the bloke I told you about,' said Tom. 'He's got good credentials. He was organiser on the ARU; helped get rid of McCormack.'

'Nice to be back in harness', Jack thought. 'Nice to have some worth.'

It was the first time Jack had been to the Toohey Forest camp, and he was impressed by what he saw. The clearing, the size of two football fields, contained a well-organised camp of huts, tents and shanties. Trees felled to make the clearing had been put to good use as framing, to which tin and sacks from the fruit market, some bearing the suppliers' names, were wired. The tents were the same as the ones he had lived in on the line: off-white canvas, 6 ft by 6 ft, placed in a row, as if waiting the arrival of a railway line. One man had gathered trunks of grass trees, unaware of how many hundreds of years they had taken to reach their height of five feet, and placed them in a circle, leaving a gap for a doorway. Saplings, interwoven with leafy branches, criss-crossed over the top to keep out the worst of the weather. And then there were tin lean-tos with just a simple swag beneath.

When Tom had first arrived at camp, he propped a piece of tin against a tree trunk and rolled out his swag of grey blanket and kapok-stuffed pillow covered with cream and grey striped ticking. Within a week, he had collected enough rocks to form three walls, cemented in place with mud from the creek bank. He scrounged tin for the roof. When winter westerlies blew a few months later, he gathered more rocks and added a chimney to the fourth wall. Saplings, bound together with twine, swung closed across the doorway.

In the centre of the campground was the communal kitchen. Stout trunks buried deep in the ground supported a tin roof some 12 feet square from which a length of guttering sloped into an open tank. A circle of stones marked the fireplace over which hung large pots and billies.

'We all know the score,' said Jack. 'In a week, the bailiff will return to Lizzie Armitage, and this time, he won't bring one police protector with him, he'll have a couple of hundred. We'll need double that number; that means every man in this camp as well as those from the Movement. Pass the word around to meet at the edge of the forest before daylight so's not to draw attention. Everyone's to keep out of sight until they get the call: no talking, no coughing, no smoking. They're the rules; any man who can't follow them needn't turn up. Tom, you take half a dozen blokes and wait inside the house, the rest of the men are to stay in the bush until the cops arrive. We need to trap them between us and the house, not the other way around. Any questions?'

'How will we know when to move?' asked one man.

'There'll be a bloke waiting nearby for a signal. As soon as the cops show, he'll come for you. Bring anything you can use: crow bars, axe handles, spades, branches, rocks. Look around camp, there's plenty of weapons here. Just remember, the cops will be armed.'

~

Lizzie sat through the night by her bed, fully clothed, listening to the steady breathing of her three kids. Cec. had only known the youngest for six months before he left. That was a year ago. She didn't blame him for going, it was the only way of finding any work, but she missed him terribly.

Afraid to sleep with a window open, she fanned their sweaty limbs with a piece of cardboard. Her daughter opened an eye, smiled, and rolled over to return to sleep.

At four o'clock came a soft tap on the door. She put her lips to the lock: 'Is that you, Tom?'

'Yes, Lizzie.'

She opened the door and once again, men filed into her kitchen.

'Off you go, Lizzie. We'll see you when it's over.'

She slipped out with her children and, in the dimness of pre-dawn, went to her kindly neighbour who waited with open door.

~

Jack slid from his bed without disturbing Mary: he did not wish to explain where he was going at 4.30 in the morning. It was still dark when he joined 400 men waiting silently among the trees on the edge of Toohey Forest.

Two streets from Lizzie's cottage, 200 policemen crouched behind paling fences while 50 mounted police approached from the east - all tense with anticipation of the arrival of the bailiff and agent. At the moment the sun's rays lit the front of the house, a truck slowed and two men jumped from the running board before it stopped. They hammered on the front door with both fists, loud enough to wake the dead. In the house next door, Lizzie hugged her kids and shuddered.

Tom opened the door and stood, arms akimbo, facing the agent, bailiff and his two offsiders.

'Mrs Armitage's not here,' he said, but they ducked under his elbows and surged into the house, grabbing furniture as they went. Tom's men fought the intruders, wrenching Lizzie's possessions from their grasp, and returned each piece to its rightful place. Tom looked up through the open front door and saw Lizzie running along the path.

'It's *my* home,' she shouted as she reached the door. 'I'm not going to hide next door while this is going on!'

Behind her, the front yard filled with police.

Tom put his index fingers to the corners of his mouth and sent a shrill whistle to the bicycle rider waiting in the next street, then pulled Lizzie into the hall and slammed the door, bolting it, trapping the bailiff and his men who now lay dazed on the kitchen floor. He handed her a crowbar: 'Here, and don't be afraid to use it'.

As she grasped the bar firmly, a window shattered behind her. She jumped. Then another window from in the bedroom. Within seconds, every window was broken, with police stepping over the sills, clearing shards of glass with their batons.

෨

At full pelt a youth rode his bicycle to Toohey Forest where he found Jack standing on a tree stump, addressing the mob. Panting, short of breath, the youth stammered: 'There's a couple of hundred cops, and they've got guns'.

'You know what to do, men,' said Jack. 'Come on, give 'em hell!'

The men rushed along Tooheys Road, shouting, weapons waving; but the wall of police prevented them from reaching Lizzie's house. Four hundred men encircled two hundred and fifty police surrounding a very small cottage.

Tom heard the Toohey Forest mob before he saw them. He also saw fear in the face of the policemen who had forced their way into the yard and house as they now turned their backs to face the threat from behind. Outside, protestors threw rocks at the police, wielded the iron bars and axe handles they had brought with them; and for a while, they were making ground.

Then came the order to fire.

Taking careful aim, the police fired upon the men, wounding but not killing. Around Jack, men fell, shot in the knee; others grabbed at their shoulders, trying to stop the pain and stem the flow of blood. Then Tom came to the front door and Jack watched as the constable who had visited Lizzie a fortnight earlier picked his mark - as instructed by his sergeant - fixed his sights on Tom's neck and squeezed the trigger. He lowered his revolver to watch as Tom's ruddy face grew pale and he fell to the ground.

The battle raged for an hour and blood flowed freely on both sides: heads, shoulders, arms, beaten and bloodied or sporting bullet wounds. Inside the house, the men continued to guard Lizzie's few possessions.

Then smoke filled the air as dried grass beneath the front fence burst into flames, blistering the remains of paint, turning the palings into charcoal.

'Tell the owner that his houses will be next!' yelled Jack as the agent beat at the flames.

By midday it was all over. Outnumbered, the police retreated to await further orders.

That afternoon the anti-eviction committee, armed with rocks, approached the agent's office in Tarragindi. By the time they left, the ground was littered with broken glass - they had delivered their message.

જ

Tom lay in hospital listening to the groans of his fellow patients, all wounded in the fight. Jack bent close to his mouth to hear his whispered words: 'The bastards have taken my voice, but they won't stop me from organising'.

He coughed and spat a blood clot into a dish.

'I guess I'll have to do the talking from now on,' said Jack.

Tom smiled his thanks.

Jack arrived home mid-afternoon, his clothes dishevelled, his hat missing, and his face smudged with soot. Mary listened, horrified, as Jack explained the events of the day.

'I can't for the life of me see why you want to visit an unemployment camp, Jack O'Leary! What will people think if they see you going there?'

'What would you have me do, Mary? Sit at home all day and read the paper? Do the crosswords? Play tennis? My brain is going to mush with all this inactivity. Can't you see, I AM BORED!'

'Better your brain to die than you. You'll be in the grave before you're 50, at this rate.'

She turned her back and busied herself preparing the evening meal. When she turned around again, Jack had left the house.

જ

Lizzie placed charred fence palings into the firebox of her stove and lit a match. She normally rationed her tea, but this was a special occasion. She pulled the iron kettle forward to boil, then sat at the kitchen table opposite Tom and Jack.

'You put up a fine fight, lass,' Jack said.

'I couldn't have done it without you, and the rest of the blokes,' she said.

Lizzie pushed a piece of paper across the table to her visitors: the reason for the celebratory cup of tea.

'I've you to thank for this, too.'

Jack read the letter aloud.

Dear Mrs. Armitage

It has come to the attention of Mr. Thomson, owner of your place of residence, that you are presently unable to pay back rent of £5. I am instructed by Mr. Thomson to inform you that he will not be pursuing this amount in the immediate future, and you are therefore at liberty to remain in residence until you can either avail yourself of this amount, or find alternative accommodation.

Sincerely

Alfred Fortescue

Real Estate Agent

Tarragindi.

'Would you really have set fire to his houses?' asked Lizzie.

'You bet your boots we would! It's the only way to let them know we mean business.'

'Remind me never to get on the wrong side of you,' she laughed.

'What'll you do now, Lizzie?' asked Jack.

'I don't want to stay here; I haven't a hope in hell of catching up on the rent. I've got an aunt in Woolloongabba who said we could stay with her for a bit. It'll be cramped - she's only got two bedrooms - but me and the kids can share a bed. At least, until Cec gets back. It's no way for a family to live, but I don't have a choice.'

'We'll give you a hand to move,' said Jack.

'Thanks, fellas. I'd appreciate that.'

Winter westerlies blew across Brisbane and people huddled in the Annerley hall to keep warm. A small flame warmed Jack's belly now that he acted as Tom's voice at these meetings. Tonight's talk, 'Unemployment and its Solution', was an attempt to explain the Douglas Credit Scheme. As far as Jack could see it was simply a readjustment of the present situation, but he was prepared to give the bloke a hearing.

As usual, the hall was filled to capacity, and it wasn't just that these meetings offered an outing; Jack could tell by the expectant faces that there was genuine interest in any ideas put forward. The present system wasn't working.

The speaker put his case: how the current financial system, with paper money owned by banks, was obsolete.

'Let me give an example,' he said. 'The price of the total output from factories for a year is over £400,000 but wages paid to people who produce the goods are only £130,000. The worker always needs more money than he gets in wages to buy the very goods he produces. If the difference between the two prices was a source of credit owned by the community, factory owners could draw on that money to cover their depreciation and running costs. So the credit would be the property of the people, instead of the banks.'

'Interesting,' Jack whispered to Tom, 'but I reckon Fred Paterson's ideas are more convincing'.

As the evening drew to a close, Jack thanked the speaker, then addressed the crowd: 'I'd like to tell you the story of the Watson family from Wellers Hill. Jim Watson worked on the gang building the road to the top of Mt Gravatt. Six months ago, his legs were crushed by a rock. Even though he was part of the relief gang paid by the government, he is now unemployed and penniless. The bailiffs will be calling at his home this week. Anyone who can help, please stay behind after the meeting.'

Every man and woman in the hall remained seated, ready to help.

❧

Chapter 15 - Hospitalised (1931)

J ack coughed through the night. This was nothing unusual, but as daylight filtered through the curtains, Mary found Jack's pillow streaked with blood and his parched lips caked with pink froth. He was incoherent and bathed in sweat.

'Madge! Jackie!' Mary yelled, frightened. They came running across the hallway into the bedroom.

'No! Don't come in!' Mary did not want them to see their father in such a state, but Jackie burst through the bedroom door, took one look, and ran out the front door. Within a few minutes he was back, taking the front stairs two at a time.

'The ambulance's on its way.'

By then Mary had changed the pillowcase and washed Jack's face, so she let the children in to see their father. She insisted on accompanying Jack to the hospital. The ambulance driver did not object.

Mary sat beside Jack's bed, surrounded by faces of the dying, in the horrible barn that was the General Hospital. She looked out at the bleakness of the place through louvred windows.

Jack was spent. He tried to smile, but the movement of his lips made them crack and bleed. She dipped a cloth in the basin of water beside his bed and wiped his forehead, averting her eyes from the spittoon with its ghastly contents. She took a jar of Vaseline from her handbag and smeared some on his lips.

'Better wash your hands,' he said - no more than a whisper.

Every day for the next month, after seeing Hazel off to school, Mary caught a bus to North Quay, then a tram to Herston to spend the day with Jack. At the weekends, Madge and Hazel, and occasionally Jackie, accompanied her. One day Mary arrived to find Jack sitting on the verandah. Mary felt the chilly breeze and demanded he be taken back inside.

'Fresh air is good for him,' said the nurse.

'Not when it makes him cough!'

But the next day when she arrived at the god-awful ward, he was outside again. After six weeks, she took him home. She knew she could look after him. At least she cared, and could give him love.

When in full health, Jack only weighed just over eight stone. He was painfully thin when he came home from hospital. Much broth and many hot lemon drinks later, he began to regain some of his lost condition.

Then, almost back to normal, Jack found a new obsession.

He and Tom attended a public meeting at the Brisbane Stadium called by a New South Wales politician, Jack Lang. It was no surprise that some of their old union mates also attended the meeting: they shared Lang's values. He was an active socialist who had long battled to break the Australian Workers Union's hold on Labor Council. As Premier of New South Wales, he passed laws lessening landlords' power over tenants who could not meet the rent. What was more important, he wished political death to Theodore who, despite the Royal Commission's findings, tenaciously clung to his position as National Treasurer. He knew no move could be made against him until the civil trial, and that was a year away.

At the rear of the stadium, Joe Collings kept his hat firmly on his head. He was less recognisable that way. Besides, with the place packed to capacity, he was almost invisible. A chill crept along his spine as the large, balding man with thick black moustache rose to his full 6'4" to address the crowd.

> I have been invited here today to outline my plan: as Premier of New South Wales, I have refused to cut government salaries, as instructed by the federal government; I have passed laws that forbid landlords to evict tenants just because they cannot pay their rent; and I insist on paying relief workers their due.

> I plan to *reduce* interest on government debts held in Australia, and to cancel interest payments to overseas bondholders. These funds will be used to revitalise industry and pump more money into the Australian economy. I am violently opposed to suggestions that wages to government employees be cut to help balance the budget.

Jack Lang paused while his audience cheered.

> I say capitalism has failed, and failed miserably, and yet we have Niemeyer deigning to pay Australia a visit in order to tell us to *depress* our wages, to cut our social services, all the while telling us to remain *loyal* to Britain. The same people who conscripted our sons and laid them in Flanders fields are now demanding more blood: the interest on the lives of our sons. I say - *Australia first!*

Lang did not need to say more. His job was done.

Collings watched as Lang moved out of the building, followed by fifty who had sat in the front few rows. He followed them, at a distance, noting the names of those marching triumphantly towards Trades Hall. As the last of Lang's supporters disappeared into the arched doorway, Collings turned and headed straight for Parliament House. He knocked on his leader's door. Forgan Smith was even more dour than usual as Joe Collings repeated the general drift of Lang's speech. But he had more news to impart.

'Guess who was sitting in the front row?'

'I'm in no mood for games, Joe. Out with it, man!'

'O'Leary.'

'That bastard from the ARU? I thought he'd be dead by now.'

'By the looks of him, it won't be long. Terribly thin and haggard. And he was with Tom Rickard from the Unemployed Workers Movement.'

'We shall have to report this to the Central Executive. We cannot have branch officials supporting this ... this monster.'

Collings smiled: 'Only too happy to oblige there'.

By that evening, a rank and file organisation had been formed in support of Jack Lang's policies. Jack O'Leary, offering his services as secretary, took down the minutes of the meeting.

The O'Leary neighbourhood had grown over the years, and now almost every second allotment contained a house. The community developed on its own, independent of the rest of Brisbane. They took turns at hosting gatherings on Saturday nights, each family bringing food to share along with songs and parodies. They formed a Saturday tennis club where the women wore white and the men, green striped blazers. Not long before Jack's previous spell in hospital, a new couple had moved into the community. The moment Mary heard the woman speak, she knew she also came from Glasgow. Mary wasn't the type to take to people straight away, but she was drawn to Jessie Anderson: as short as herself at just over five feet, but with dark wavy hair.

The two women, well on their way to being friends, were on the sidelines watching a men's double match one Saturday when Jessie said: 'I've been wondering how Jack is now'.

Mary had taken great pains to ensure the state of Jack's health was not general knowledge in the neighbourhood. She looked at Jessie, puzzled.

'Jackie used our telephone to call the ambulance.'

'Oh, I didn't know that. He's very well at the moment, thank you.' She didn't want to alarm this new-found friend - people were afraid of TB.

As their friendship deepened, the two families visited regularly and Jessie and Mary lunched at Finney's cafeteria each Friday and enjoyed the city shops.

ॐ

Jack and Mary were taking tea on the front verandah one afternoon when Madge came rushing in the front gate. Mary knew immediately something had happened: Madge never rushed. She puffed up the stairs. 'I've got a job, starting Monday.'

'That's great news!' said Jack.

'What? Where?'

Madge sat down on the wooden slatted chair to catch her breath.

'It's at Coles, in the city. I'll be working at the perfumery.'

Mary knew Madge would be happy with that job, it had class.

'The woman in charge, Mrs Barry, said she got sick of the sight of me always hanging around, asking for work. I'm to replace a woman who's leaving to get married.'

'Well, congratulations, Darling. I knew something would turn up eventually.' Mary poured her a cup of tea to celebrate, but did not look forward to days without her companion.

ॐ

August brought the cold dry westerly winds and with it, a return of Jack's TB. Mary knew it was coming. He lost his appetite, then followed restless nights of fighting sweat-drenched sheets. Within a couple of days he was back in hospital. Again the daily visits. Again he was placed on the cold verandah with no sun.

George Rymer visited him one weekend, horrified to see the hospital ward.

'Surely you can get him out of here,' he whispered to Mary. Jack opened his eyes just enough to see: 'What're you two whispering about?' They waited for a coughing bout to pass.

'This place is so depressing. Surely you can find somewhere better to go when you're so sick?'

'I could go to Rosemount, but the army won't admit my lung condition's got anything to do with the war.'

'That's a lot of rot! Of course it has. How long since you've been in touch with them?'

'Nineteen thirty. When the union re-opened the district offices, I applied for an increase in my pension, which they refused. They'll accept responsibility for the deafness, but the chest's an entirely different matter.'

George turned to Mary. 'I think you should go and see them at Repat. Maybe you could use your womanly wiles. I'll come with you, if you think it would help.'

If Mary was to appeal to the Repatriation Department, she would have to discuss Jack's submersion after being torpedoed, and neither she nor Jack wanted George to know he had been court-martialled for desertion.

'You're very kind, George, but I can handle it myself.'

George drove her home, and as he helped her from the front seat, he urged, 'Please try to get him into Rosemount, Mary. This place will be the death of him.'

'I will, George. Thanks for the ride home.'

That afternoon, she wrote to the Department of Repatriation, Brisbane, asking for an urgent appointment. A week later she sat opposite the Deputy Commissioner as he silently read through Jack's war record. Eventually he closed the file and leaned forward, interlocking his fingers as he rested on his elbows.

'You're married to a spirited man, Mrs O'Leary.'

She searched his face for some indication whether she was facing friend or foe. He leant back in his chair, then smiled. She relaxed.

'There's no doubt that Private O'Leary is now suffering as a result of exposure. The trouble is, he was a member of the Royal Navy when the *Boravia* went down.'

Her heart sank.

'Then there's nothing that can be done?'

'I'm not saying that, I'm saying this complicates matters. Under normal circumstances, I wouldn't waste my time trying to help a deserter; however Mr O'Leary is not your normal deserter. It's clear from the transcript of his Court Martial that he tried to get *into* the fighting, not *out* of it. He has good referees, and they hold him in high regard. After all, Australia's part of the British Commonwealth and our men were fighting for England.'

He stood and extended a hand to Mary.

'Leave it with me, Mrs O'Leary. I'll see what can be done.'

Mary brought Jack home two weeks later. The next day a letter arrived from the Deputy Commissioner instructing Jack to report to Rosemount Military Hospital at Windsor and register as an outpatient. And at the bottom of the letter:

I am also recommending the Royal Navy considers the issue of compensation for Private O'Leary's diminished state of health.

 ❧

Rosemount Military Hospital was everything the Brisbane General Hospital wasn't. Behind what had once been a grand home, timber wards sprawled across six acres of garden, facing east, sloping gently towards Breakfast Creek.

The matron in charge of the TB ward welcomed Jack and Mary and showed them around with pride. The men were just as ill as those in the General, but they exhibited an air of hope. Sunlight streamed onto the beds and, with verandahs on all sides, no matter what the time of day the patients could find a patch of sun among the shrubs planted in pots on the verandah.

The Matron then introduced them to the lung specialist who thoroughly examined Jack. He took the time to answer their questions:

'My main concern is the family,' said Jack. 'We're taking all the precautions we can, but it's a constant worry.'

'I can understand that. The fact is, every time an infected person sneezes or coughs he releases bacillus into the air. The good news is that while a lot of people breathe in the bacteria, it mostly remains inactive. Think of it as a scab covering a sore. While it's encased, it will not harm.

'It's only when there's a general breakdown in a person's health that the bacteria break free and affect the lungs. In your case, Jack, your recurrent bronchitis would have been sufficient to set things going.

'Take as much fresh air and exercise as you can, and make sure you have a nutritious diet.'

'No question about that,' said Jack, grinning at Mary. 'She feeds me as if I'm a starving orphan!'

'Good. Wholesome home cooking is just what you need. The other good news is that there are experiments underway with sulphur and penicillin. So far, they've been ineffective against tuberculosis, but the promise is there.'

For the first time since Jack's diagnosis, they felt there was hope.

≈

Chapter 16 - Expelled (1931-1936)

J ack tore open the envelope with the ALP stamp on the top left-hand corner, totally unprepared for its contents.

Dear Mr O'Leary

It has come to the notice of the Queensland Central Executive of the Australian Labor Party that you have become involved in an organisation supporting the ideology of one Jack Lang, Premier of New South Wales.

The Executive decided at a meeting held last night that it sees no alternative but to suspend you from your position as Secretary of the Annerley branch of this organisation until you disassociate yourself from the abovementioned organisation.

Signed

J.S. Collings.

A month later, Jack was expelled from the Labor Party to which he had devoted his entire adult life.

Now outside the ALP, Jack acted as scrutineer during the Federal Elections in November 1931. Jackie helped out during these elections too, but not in a way that pleased his father. His seventeen-year-old son had a girlfriend living in South Brisbane. She had a brother, a doctor, standing for Parliament. He belonged to the Tories.

'How can a son of mine hand out how-to-vote cards for the Tories?'

Jackie looked along the dinner table at Jack: 'Being a son of yours doesn't chain me to your beliefs'.

On Election Day, Hazel took the suitcase full of sandwiches and thermos of tea to the voting hall. That night Mary joined Jack at the hall to hear of Prime Minister Scullin's defeat, and Joseph Lyons of the United Australia Party taking his place. Four ministers had lost their seats, one of them, Ted Theodore, was defeated by a Lang candidate.

A month later, Jack Lang successfully moved that Theodore, one-time Premier of Queensland and Federal Treasurer, be expelled from the Australian Labor Party.

June 1932 saw a return of the ALP to government in Queensland under the leadership of Forgan Smith. Again, Jack acted as scrutineer and Hazel carried the suitcase of sandwiches to the hall at lunchtime.

â¶

When Jackie turned eighteen, he decided to move into journalism in earnest. He enrolled at the Queensland University to undertake a Bachelor of Arts degree, and progressed from reader to journalist at *The Daily Standard*.

As 1932 drew to a close, Jack said goodbye to his friend Fred Paterson who, early that year, had married Kathleen - a tall, elegant, gentle woman with striking dark hair. Now Fred was needed in north Queensland to defend the rights of the Italian cane-cutters.

Jack's health seesawed from one year's end to the next. When he was well, he put his full strength into the Unemployed Workers Movement and support for Jack Lang. When he was ill, he was very ill. At times he was in Rosemount Hospital for months at a time.

Each day Mary caught a bus to town, then a tram to Windsor. Each weekend Hazel accompanied her. Jack's frame grew skeletal.

During the summer, they retreated to Strongarra where Jack regained some of his lost strength.

At the end of 1935, Hazel won a scholarship to attend Business College the following year.

~

Frank Ryan swung his left fist into the soft belly of his mother-in-law and stepped over her crumpling bulk into the small cottage: 'Gwen! Where the fuck are you. Gwennie!'

On the table, three plates held the scattered remains of breakfast. A fly circled a piece of netting covering a half-filled jug of milk. He pulled aside the curtain over the bedroom door; nothing but a double and single bed, neatly made. The ripple of a child's laugh floated in through the louvres above the stove alcove. Frank sprang towards the back door.

In the pocket-handkerchief back yard a boy with brown hair ran in circles around the clothesline prop, chased by his mother. The baby in the dog-eared photo Frank had kept in his shirt pocket for the past four years had grown. The boy stopped when he saw the stranger standing on the top step. His mother grabbed him around the waist: 'Gotcha!' then followed her son's stare, and instinctively grabbed his hand and pulled him to her. Frank sank to the step, coming to grips with his emotions.

Gwen lifted her son onto her hip: 'Gees, Frank, what'd you come here for?'

He pulled a tobacco pouch from his pocket, rolled a cigarette, lit up, all the time staring at his wife.

'We're okay without you. Things are nice here, Frank.'

He crushed the cigarette into his hand.

'You're my wife, and you're coming with me.'

'Coming with you! Where to? You got somewhere to live?'

'We'll get somewhere.'

'You got a job?'

'I'll get one.'

'Come back when you do!'

She climbed the steps and as she pushed past Frank, his son's feet brushed his shoulder. He waited for Gwen's scream as she saw her mother sitting in the front doorway, clutching her stomach.

'You bastard! What've you done?'

'She wouldn't let me in.'

'Get outa here, Frank Ryan. Just get out!'

His fist splintered the weathered front door as he left the cottage.

༐

Mr. J. O'Leary

154 Venner Road

Yeronga.

30th September, 1936

Dear Mr. O'Leary,

After due consideration, it has been decided to award you a full pension for injuries sustained during the Great War. It is acknowledged that as a result of your exposure following the sinking of the Boravia, *your lungs suffered damage to the extent they contributed to your contracting tuberculosis.*

A pension of £5 per week will be paid to you, commencing November this year. This includes part-pension of £3 you are currently receiving on behalf of the Australian Government.

It is further considered this pension was due from the time of your diagnosis with tuberculosis. Please find enclosed cheque for £832 in payment of arrears.

Deputy Commissioner,

Department of Repatriation,

Brisbane.

'Instead of Strongarra, let's go to Mount Tamborine,' said Mary, 'we can afford to now'.

'To hell with Tamborine, we'll go to Sydney!'

'That's a bit extravagant, isn't it?'

'Mary O'Leary, we've been to hell and back these past few years. I think we deserve a bit of extravagance.'

The following Friday, over lunch at Finneys, Mary shared their good news with Jessie who immediately responded: 'Let's go and get your fortune read. I know a clairvoyant at Red Hill, she's very good.'

'Oh, I don't know. What if she tells me something I don't want to hear?'

'Just say you don't believe it,' said Jessie.

'But you know how superstitious I am. I'm afraid I *will* believe it.'

'Nonsense!' said Jessie. 'We're going.' She waved to the waitress for the bill.

'She might not be home,' Mary said as they knocked on the front door. She felt nervous about this harebrained idea.

A very normal looking woman of about fifty opened the door.

'Hello Mrs Strongman. May I introduce my friend Mrs O'Leary? We were wondering if you'd be able to do a reading this afternoon.'

'Yes, of course. Please come in and make yourselves welcome. I'm just about to make a pot of tea.'

Around a circular table covered with a thick tapestry cloth, they drank tea, ate cake, then Mrs Strongman removed the lid from a polished wooden box and withdrew a pack of Tarot cards. She passed them to Mary.

'Handle them for a while, will you please, Mrs O'Leary?'

Mary was no stranger to cards, she and Jack played each evening when he was at home. She shuffled the large cards, then handed them back to Mrs Strongman.

'Now, cut the pack please.'

As the cards appeared, one by one, on the table, Mary felt the mood of the room change: this woman told her she had three children; she told her she had led a full and eventful life; she told her only one of her children would have children. Then she covered her mouth in shock.

'What is it? What do you see?'

'Oh God! It's too terrible. I can't say.'

'Come now, Mrs Strongman,' said Jessie, 'you can't leave it at that!'

'It's, it's your husband. Oh, Mrs O'Leary, I see a death.'

'There must be a mistake,' said Jessie, trying to ease the situation. 'Mr O'Leary is very ill. That is what you can see.'

'Oh no, dear - I never make mistakes. It's here very clearly.'

'How long? I mean, when?' Mary asked, but she didn't want to hear the answer.

'November.'

'Not this year, though,' said Jessie, still trying to ward off the spell.

'I'm horribly afraid it is this year.'

Mary felt great hatred welling up inside her for this fortune teller. She rose from the table, grabbed her hat and bag, and left the house, tears streaming down her face. She was halfway up the street before Jessie caught up with her.

'No! No! She doesn't know what she's saying. How can she say such things!'

On the 1st of November Mary waited. Try as she might, she could not rid her head of Mrs Strongman's words. She told Madge, but no one else in the family knew.

November turned into a beautiful month. Jack booked their passage to Sydney on the *Manunda* and convinced Mary that their children were now old enough to look after themselves for three weeks.

The ship took two days to reach Sydney. After all the years, it felt as if they were on their honeymoon. Upon calm seas, they played deck quoits and watched the dolphins ride the bow wave. In the evenings they leant against the rail and sang to each other. Mary fell in love with her husband all over again.

They stayed at a hotel at Bondi, walked along the beach, their shoes in their hands, arms linked.

The *Manunda* returned to Hamilton Wharf three weeks later, and their three children were waiting for them. Jackie had borrowed a motorcar for the day, and drove them home in style.

As Mary turned November's calendar to December, she breathed a deep sigh of relief: Mrs Strongman had been wrong.

Chapter 17 - A woman screams (1936)

In the corner of the private lounge of the Bellevue Hotel Premier Forgan Smith leaned towards his companion, speaking in lowered tones.

'We need to keep our eye on the Port Kembla situation. The wharfies are agitating for a union-controlled roster system, and the Brisbane mob are threatening to come out on strike in support.'

'Who are the chief stirrers?' asked Joe Collings.

'Tom Rickard and Cec. Armitage. Real trouble makers. They used to work in the railways until '29. Then Rickard headed the Unemployed Workers Movement. Now they're both on the wharves. They need to be taught a lesson before this gets out of hand. We can't afford trouble on the waterfront, not while the economy's still on its knees.'

'Consider it done, Bill.'

☙

The acrid smell of old smoke rose through the decking of Victoria Bridge, mingling with the late-afternoon Saturday traffic. Frank

Ryan swung down the bank beneath the bridge and took up his place by the fire. In the few months he had been back in Brisbane, he had manipulated the poor sods around the fire drum until he now sat on the far side of the fire, constantly on the lookout for cops. Manipulating his way back into Gwen's life was not so easy. He had only managed to see his kid three times, and only by waiting outside his mother-in-law's cottage until Gwen had come down the stairs on her way to somewhere. But she was weakening, he was sure of it. Still, there was not much sense in looking for work or paying rent on a place until he was dead sure. Now, with the summer settling in, he was happy enough camping on the riverbank. Most of the old blokes had disappeared - probably dead - but his mate Joe Esler was still here.

'Got a job on tonight, Joe.'

'Yeah? Who?'

'Couple of wharfies.'

'Hope they're not big 'uns.'

'No, just average, it'll be a pushover. They're always at the Grand on a Saturday arvo. We'll head up there in about an hour.'

'Okay.'

&

Mary took care pressing her dress, fanning out the circular skirt, ironing the bias cut smooth. The white chain-stitched scalloped pattern around the hem of the capped sleeves contrasted well with the royal blue rayon. She was proud of her work.

This evening was special: she was to meet Jessie at the Workers Education Association Dramatic Society to see *The Black Eye* by Scottish playwright James Bridie, and she wanted to look her best. Just before lunch, Jack came into the kitchen, dressed for town, carrying his blue serge coat and felt hat.

'Where're you going?' Mary asked.

'I'm meeting Tom and Cec. at the Anzac Club. England's batting today, and they're broadcasting the match.'

'But you're taking Hazel to the pictures tonight. I asked you weeks ago.'

'I haven't forgotten. I'll be home in plenty of time to take her.' He took his watch from his waistcoat pocket. 'I'd better get going or I'll miss the tram.'

He poked his head around Hazel's door on the way down the hall: 'See you at six'.

❧

Even at five-thirty, the air held the stickiness of a Brisbane summer's day. In the bar beyond the open door, the tinkle of glass on glass cut through the hum of men's voices. Frank scratched at the rash on the back of his neck, then flicked the flakes of skin from beneath his broken fingernails. He looked along the laneway towards Elizabeth Street as a vehicle chugged into view then moved on, leaving a plume of blue smoke. He nodded at the silhouette of Joe, on lookout beside some empty kegs. If there was a breeze, it couldn't find its way through the laneway that ran beside Grand Central Hotel, linking Queen Street to Elizabeth Street.

Frank's back itched. He rubbed it on the wall of rough bricks, buying a few moments relief. Beads of blood seeped through the discoloured cotton of his brown shirt where it snagged on the mortar.

Someone laughed aloud inside the bar, someone else shouted and cigarette smoke, caught in the daylight, curled into the laneway. Frank patted his shirt pocket, then remembered that he smoked his last cigarette that morning. Frustrated, he tore at his neck again and cursed as he drew blood.

A middle-aged man merged from the doorway to the bar and turned towards the toilets further down the laneway. He saw the young man leaning against the far wall and nodded gidday. Frank's eyes focussed and his mouth became dry as he stood to attention. He beckoned Joe and began working his fingers into a fist.

❧

At six o'clock Mary dressed for her outing. Madge, who had spent the afternoon putting the finishing touches to a dress she was making, modelled it for Hazel and Mary. Dusky pink taffeta with a peplum that gave the illusion of hips to her thin body.

Mary and Hazel leant on the kitchen window, watching Madge walk up Venner Road to catch the tram. Six-thirty, and Jack was still not home. Mary looked at Hazel: fourteen and stood up by her father.

'Oh, go and get dressed. I'll change and we'll go to town.'

Furious, Mary took off her theatre gown, threw it on the bed and changed into street clothes. She held Hazel's hand as they walked to catch the tram - small comfort.

'Don't feel too badly, Mum. I enjoy looking at the shops just as much as going to the pictures. Daddy and I can go to the pictures next week.'

In these days of low income, window-shopping on a Saturday night was a popular pastime. The store managers knew this, and the city department stores competed with each other. The shops weren't open, but each window was brightly lit and beautifully displayed. Mary and Hazel joined the crowds walking Queen Street. They lingered over a malted milk at the milk bar near North Quay, then walked the full length of the shops down the left side of Queen Street. The only disturbance was a small scuffle outside Allan & Starks' store when two policemen marched a young man away between them. Mary looked at Hazel and cast her eyes skywards in disgust. They passed the paperboy on the T & G Corner, waving the Telegraph, shouting the headlines of the afternoon edition, trying to sell his papers.

They ambled the full length of the shops in Queen Street, admiring the clothes and furniture they could not afford, then crossed Queen Street and window-gazed down the other side. As they passed the T & G Corner on their return, the paperboy's chant had changed to that of the evening edition's headlines: 'Man killed in Queen Street! Man killed in Queen Street!'

Mary stopped, grabbed Hazel's arm: 'It couldn't be Dad. He's never in Queen Street.'

She knew his path well. He always walked up Elizabeth Street from the Anzac Club to catch the tram at North Quay.

Again, she reassured Hazel: 'It couldn't be Dad. He wouldn't be in Queen Street.'

Feeling uneasy, they returned to North Quay and caught the tram home. A young lass who lived nearby was on the tram too, and they walked together down Venner Road. She said goodnight and peeled off at her intersection.

From nowhere a little white fluffy dog joined them and wove his way between their feet. Mary tried to shoo him away, but he kept getting in front of her. As they crossed the side street, they saw a man walking towards them.

'It's probably your father! If he's come to apologise, it's too late!'

But as the form grew nearer, they saw that it was Jackie.

❧

Somewhere, a woman screams.

Mary feels her son's arms around her shoulders, gently steering her home.

The woman screams again, closer this time.

Mary closes her eyes; hears her son's voice beside her ear: 'Run home and open the house, Hazel.'

Hazel's shoes beat out a rhythm on the bitumen, growing fainter -

Tick-tock-tick-tock goes the little French clock.

Please someone, make that woman stop screaming!

Mary stops her screaming. Now everything is deathly quiet as they reach the front gate. The door is wide open and there are people all around. Jessie places an arm around her shoulders and steers her towards her bedroom.

Mary lies on her bed. The whole world goes black.

❧

Morning broke. Mary lay still, but she wasn't asleep. It had not been a dream. Jackie knocked on her bedroom door.

'Yes?' Her voice was barely audible.

He opened it, and entered. She could tell he hadn't been asleep. His eyes told her he'd done a good deal of crying.

'Where are Madge and Hazel?'

'They're in bed.'

Still in her street clothes, Mary got up from the bed and crossed the hall to her daughters' bedroom. They were both in Madge's bed. Madge looked at her across Hazel and, withdrawing her arm from beneath her sister's sleeping head, joined Mary and Jackie in the kitchen.

'Maybe it isn't Jack,' Mary said to Jackie.

'It is, Mum. I had to go to the morgue last night and identify him.'

'When?'

'Before you came home.'

'How did you know. I mean, who told you?'

'When I came home last night, Old Bob from next door was waiting in his front yard. He said: "Well, you're father's dead, the police have been here, you'd better do something about it".'

Hazel appeared at the kitchen door, her eyes swollen. Without words, she sat at the table. Jackie continued.

'I went around to Andy's house. I didn't know what else to do. He drove me into town.'

'Was he badly injured?' Mary asked.

'No. There's just a bruise and some swelling on his right cheek.'

A car pulled up outside.

'Oh God, no. Whoever it is, tell them I can't see anyone.'

Jackie went out, and Mary heard him speaking to Tom and Cec. Shaken from her trance, she hurried to the front door. These two friends of Jack had been frequent visitors. Today they seemed like strangers.

'How are you, Mary?'

'Please, come in.'

She led them into the kitchen.

'Were you there?' she asked.

'Yes,' they answered in unison.

Jackie, sitting in his father's chair, said: 'I think we all need to know exactly what happened'.

'We left the Anzac Club at four o'clock and called into the Grand for drink. Like we always do.'

'Had Jack been drinking?'

'Two shandies. That's all,' replied Cec.

'Go on,' Mary said, nodding to Tom.

'We were talking about the cricket match and things like the wharfies' roster. Jack said he had to get home to take Hazel to the pictures, and we left him finishing his shandy while we went to the lavatory in the laneway.'

'I came out of the lav first,' said Cec, 'and noticed two young blokes hanging round near the door to the bar. Bad types, I've seen them there before. One of them, a cocky little runt, came over and asked me for a cigarette. I told him I didn't have any - even apologised for the fact. Next thing I know he says: "You bastards never have any", and he started laying into me. Kept hitting me around the head. I thought I was going to pass out.'

'When I saw what this cove was doing to Cec,' said Tom, 'I raced over to help and the other one, the dark one, came at me. He knocked me down, but I got up and was ready for a fight. The yardman came out of the toilet at that point and broke us up. He picked up my hat and handed it to me when this bloke rushed at me again.'

'I got up as Tom was knocked down,' continued Cec. 'That's when Jack came out to see what the ruckus was all about.'

He paused, then he continued.

'The bloke who punched me walked up to Jack and said:

"You keep out of this O'Leary. It's got nothing to do with you." A second later, he punched Jack on the jaw. Jack didn't even look like he was going to fight him!'

Mary wondered how the frail seven-stone body of her husband would have been capable of fighting anyone.

'He fell - just like a pack of cards. He lay there against a stack of wood. I knew he was gone.'

Cec. stopped, his head was bowed. 'You poor man', thought Mary.

'They got him, you know - the joker who did it. His name's Ryan. They arrested him outside Allan & Starks an hour after he bolted down the laneway.'

࿓

Sunday afternoon, Mary stood before the open coffin and looked at Jack, all dressed up in bib-and-tucker. His freckles stood out. She kissed his lips. The smell of incense would forever smell of death to her after that day.

࿓

'When I die, I want to be cremated. No bloody grave and tombstone, thank you very much! If there's no crematorium in Brisbane then send me to Rockhampton.'

There was a crematorium in Brisbane. Mt Thompson had not long been opened. The only man of religion Jack had any time for throughout his life was the padre he had befriended in the trenches of France. Each respected the other, despite coming from opposing sides of a faith. Mary liked to think Jack would have approved of her choice of minister for the ceremony. He spoke reverently of Jack's atheism. His union mates were all there.

As they left the building, Tom turned around and looked up at the smoking chimney. Mary's eyes followed his.

'There he goes,' said Tom, 'on his way to organise the angels'.

࿓

POSTSCRIPT

Francis John Ryan was charged with the murder of John Laurence O'Leary, invalid pensioner, aged 48 years, on 5 December 1936. Before judge and jury, he was found guilty on 15 April 1937.

⁊

On 27 April, Mr Justice E A Douglas sentenced Ryan to two years' Hard Labour: to be released at the end of nine months on his own bond of £25, to be of good behaviour for the balance of the period.

Before sentencing Ryan, Justice Douglas made this comment on the Social System:

> Your condition is as much due to the social system under which we are working - neglecting to provide opportunities for young men - as it is to yourself. I do not intend to allow you to wander about the streets of Brisbane as you have been wandering for some months or years. I intend to keep you in gaol for some little time to break your present associations. If you can satisfy the authorities that you will be able to get some regular employment, I would be prepared to recommend that the sentence be further reduced.

Ryan was released after giving assurance he would move to Sydney, where he said a job awaited him. But on 16 December 1938, while still under a good behaviour bond, Ryan (aka John Joseph Keenan) was arrested in Bundaberg, Queensland for brawling with a patron of the Grand Hotel. He was still unemployed and had served just nine months of his sentence for the murder of Jack O'Leary. The Solicitor General said no good purpose would be served by pursuing Ryan and recommended no action be taken.

Such a lenient sentence for a person found guilty of murder was surprising. Even manslaughter would attract a more severe sentence. Was someone looking after Francis John Ryan?

~

Mary never remarried and died from a diabetes-related illness in 1956. She was 69. Madge died of a stroke in 1999, aged 83. Jackie, who changed his name by deed poll to Shawn, went to the Second World War as a war correspondent. He became a respected journalist, published author and poet. He rarely saw his mother and sisters after leaving for the war. He died in 1992.

~

Hazel married Floyd Jacobsen in 1941 and is still very much alive. She had two daughters: my sister Beverley, and myself.

~

Fred Paterson devoted his life defending the rights of Australian workers, in particular, Italian cane-cutters of north Queensland. In 1944, he made history by being elected to the seat of Bowen - the only Communist ever to be elected to Parliament in Australia. Then, on St Patrick's Day 1948, during a bitter dispute between the ARU and the Hanlon-led Queensland ALP, Fred

> ... saw a plain clothes detective bashing into one of the members of the procession, with a baton. So I went over and called out to him to stop. He took no notice of me so I decided that I would take notes to refresh my memory. I had just lifted my pen to write on my legal brief which I had in my hand, when I was struck down by a policeman's baton, and taken unconscious to the ambulance.

~

Two years later, in 1950, the Labor Party gerrymandered his Bowen electorate out of existence. He moved to Sydney where he established a practice specialising in Industrial Law. He died on 7 October 1977 leaving his beloved Kathleen and two sons.

Bill McCormack, exposed as a liar to his party and the Australian people, never re-entered politics, but became a relatively successful businessman. He died, still a bachelor, in 1947.

Ted Theodore never quite lived down the Mungana scandal. In 1935, a resolution at the Metropolitan Conference of the ALP was carried one hundred to two that Theodore not be re-admitted to the Party. In subsequent years, he built a large newspaper empire with Frank Packer and a mining empire with John Wren. He died in 1950.

There are still people who will earn a quick dollar by carrying out unsavoury deeds for corrupt people in positions of power.